A SCHOOL IN THE HILLS

Katharine Stewart

THE MERCAT PRESS
EDINBURGH

First published in 1996 by Mercat Press
at James Thin, 53 South Bridge
Edinburgh EH1 1YS

ISBN 1873644 54X

Set in Gill Sans and Garamond 10/12 point
at Mercat Press
Printed and bound by Bell & Bain Ltd, Glasgow

Dedication

Remembering Hilda and Richard, my mother and father
and my first teachers, who showed me flowers and birds,
an island and the sea, pictures and books and
the pattern of the stars

Contents

Illustrations

Preface

Schooling, in the literate sense, has been going on in these hills just beyond the Great Glen for close on 1,500 years. In earlier times the children would have been taught the basic skills for survival. The coming of Columba and his followers to the west in the year 563 brought the beginning of book learning, of the acquisition of the alphabet, of reading and of writing.

The Great Glen forms part of the long diagonal split which opened a gateway from the west. It has been called 'the valley of the Saints', for many holy men, including Saint Moluag from Applecross, travelled it in their mission to the northern Picts. Columba came this way on his journey to Inverness to parley with King Brude. It was not an easy journey, made in frail craft which had to be carried overland between the lochs. There were mishaps and encounters with unfriendly people. But at last, some ten miles short of their objective, the 'palace' of King Brude, they stopped on a green shelf by the shore of Loch Ness. It was a good place, looking into the morning sun, with fresh water cascading over rocky pools. Here, as the years passed, a settlement grew and teaching flourished.

Though the records are blank during the turbulent times of invasions and civil war, there is no doubt that learning went on in the precincts of nearby Priories and Abbeys, till the emergence of schools and the appointment of scholarly men as teachers in the fourteenth century. It is more than likely that boys from these hills would have attended institutions such as the 'schule' in Beauly and later on the grammar school in Inverness. A distance of ten miles was not considered an impediment. And they would have spread their learning among their friends.

From the late eighteenth century there are records enough, of teachers, their salaries, the numbers of scholars, the joys and problems of the whole drama of education as it was played out in many parts of the Highlands. The people of this particular region have been fortunate in having had access to learning from the earliest times. There have been many periods of darkness, but the lamp has never been extinguished:

it still shines out through the generations of pupils of the last school at Abriachan, who have gone on to work as teachers, doctors, ministers, engineers and lawyers in many parts of the world.

The school has closed its doors now and today's children must go elsewhere to be taught. Yet there is still the aura of learning about the place, not only of book learning, but of learning, as Columba's scholars learnt, about bird and beast, rock, tree and flower, how to cherish and respect them and so learn to keep the planet alive.

In this, the 300th year since the passing of the great Act 'for the Settlement of Schools', I thought it might be interesting to see how the provisions of this Act worked out in the Highlands generally and in the area of Abriachan, by Loch Ness, in particular. I looked at the state of education prior to the Act and the measures that stemmed from it and gradually a wider view began to emerge.

In the telling of the story of learning in these hills I have found help in many sources: the archives of the Highland Council, the Scottish Record Office in Edinburgh and the Educational Resource Centre in Inverness; the *Transactions* of the Gaelic Society of Inverness, those of the Inverness Field Club and of other learned societies in the Inverness Library. The recollections of many former teachers, pupils and other people connected with schooling have been invaluable. I should like to thank the Highland Council for permission to include extracts from the Log Book of Abriachan School. My special thanks go to Mr Steward, archivist for the Highland Council, for his ever-friendly help and encouragement. And, of course, to Tom Johnstone of the Mercat Press, who has nurtured the story from the start.

Chapter One

When we arrived in the Highlands to work a croft, a number of years ago, the schooling of a small daughter, then just three years old, was not an immediate topic of discussion, though the subject was always alive at the back of our minds. We knew there were schools in the neighbourhood, good primary schools, staffed by good Highland teachers. We assumed there always would be.

It was November. The priorities were to have some basic alterations to the house finished, to get the water in, to assess what needed to be done outside—fencing, draining and so on—so that real work could begin in the spring. We had an early fall of snow. We trailed a sledge to collect eggs from a kindly neighbour. We learned to stock the larder to tide us over the days, or weeks, when the grocer's van couldn't get through the drifts. We were all learning, all the time.

Neighbouring children, orphans brought up on the crofts, came, shyly at first, to play. Play was a treat when there was so often a job to be done—collecting sticks, fetching water, bringing in the cow. They soon became good friends. Their guardians, our crofter neighbours, became good friends, too, and by new year we were visiting their homes and enjoying many a ceilidh.

In the winter months that followed, the short daylight hours were mostly filled with basic outdoor chores—clearing snow, collecting and cutting firewood. But there was always time for the radio. 'Music and Movement' made us think there were at least twenty children capering round the kitchen. 'Science and the Community' and many other schools programmes might bewilder slightly, but could certainly stretch keen young minds. Teatime on Saturdays meant a capering by all of us to the sounds of Scottish dance music. There were regular reading-aloud sessions from colourful books, print and picture easily followed by finger and eye, and within the year Helen had learnt to read on her own.

I remembered my own childhood and its early learning. My father, a history and English master, was teaching in a remote part of the country. There was no primary school within miles, but the house was full of books and my brother and I would scrabble about among them on wet days, when our main preoccupations out-of-doors were curtailed. My mother was a linguist and occasionally she and my father would hold brief conversations in what was to us a strange and mysterious tongue. Gradually the words 'pas devant les enfants' and the sudden cessation of an interchange in English gave us the delicious sensation of having been on the verge of some revelation about one of the intriguing things of our world. Thereafter my mother taught us many fascinating phrases which was the start of a continuing absorption of everything Gallic—language, and culture in the widest sense.

These memories helped me in my new role as educator. There were books always to hand, pencils and paints. Cardboard boxes were an endless source of pleasure. The big ones made boats and houses, the small ones could be shaped and coloured and made into an enormous variety of artefacts.

With our third winter under way, life on the croft settling down, we came to a decision about schooling. It happened that, geographically, we were within the catchment area of two schools—one in Abriachan, one in the neighbouring parish at Glenconvinth. At that particular time the pupils in Abriachan numbered only six—five boys and a girl. Prospects of companionship for Helen did not seem good. Bertha, who was fostered by our good neighbours the Macleans, went to Glenconvinth. She had already told us a lot about the school, the teachers, the girls, the games they played. It seemed there would be an easy entrée there for a very new girl.

One afternoon in late January, when winter was wearing on, the light was strengthening and new beginnings were in the air, we set off, the three of us, to see the school over the hill, and, we hoped, to meet the couple who ran it. We took the way that Helen would take—along the edge of the lower field, down the heather slope to the burn, over the clear brown water on stepping-stones, past the Macleans' house, where Bertha would meet her, and up another heathery slope to the stile and the road. For half a mile along this road our eyes never left the sky to the west, where hill after hill, still streaked with snow, was etched against the blue. A solitary buzzard came planing high overhead. The good day would have brought him out prospecting. Nearer hand the little scattered houses lay snugly in the pattern of their fields, thin plumes of smoke rising from the chimneys. To sense this landscape as a child would surely mean a lifelong love of stillness and space, we thought. Then it was down to the shelter of roadside birch and

2

alder and the sight of the school building, with the branches of a great oak tapping on its window.

We stood there together for a few moments, listening. There was the sound of an adult voice, a firm but friendly tone, then young voices in turn, confident and calm, responding. It sounded like a good learning atmosphere. Minutes later, a door opened and children of Helen's age emerged, giving us shy smiles as they scampered off to their nearby homes. When she had helped the last one on with coat and school-bag, a lady appeared. She was smiling, too. 'This is Helen?' she said. 'Bertha has told me about her. Come on in. My wee ones are off home now. I'll get my husband to speak to you.' She disappeared into the 'big' room to supervise while her husband came to greet us. His voice, like his wife's, had all the welcoming and sensitive cadences of the West. No child could be in better hands than these, we felt. Would it be in order for Helen to come to his school, we queried, when Abriachan school was actually nearer? He smiled. 'You come to school tomorrow, Helen' he said.

So that was happily settled. It was arranged that she would start as soon as the worst of winter was over and would come three days a week until Easter. We made our way home as the sky was fading and a handful of pale stars was starting to shine. A hare streaked across the road ahead, a roe deer was barking excitedly, in alarm, among the pines. Hills, trees, roe deer, a great silent bird—surely vital elements in education, to supplement the three Rs, we thought. Reaching the stile, we caught sight of our home again, another small stone house in its pattern of fields. Soon we'd have the smoke rising from the chimney and cups of hot tea on the table. We would be able to see Helen coming home in winter dusks. The link between home and school was forged.

Chapter
Two

Next day Bertha appeared with a book from the school library, lent by the teacher. This thoughtful gesture of welcome was much appreciated by us all.

The spell of bright, calm weather and the lengthening of the light raised our spirits to the point of imagining spring wafting in on a westerly from somewhere beyond Strathconon. But of course we knew this was only a dream, a chuckle in the face of the unknown. Sure enough, within a week the wind was roaring out of the north, not the west, bearing the mark of Siberia. The numbing ferocity of this wind was such that to venture outside meant progressing with the utmost wariness, one step at a time, half bent, holding on to fence posts, till the steading was reached. Peering from the shelter of the byre we checked the damage—one huge old rowan down, the roof off the hen-house, scattered debris everywhere.

During the days of storm that followed there was nothing for it but to stay indoors, once the essential outside chores were done. It was a time for reading, writing, inventing fascinating ploys. The shrieking of the wind under the slates, the moaning in the chimney, became as much a part of life as the bubbling up of the porridge-pot for breakfast in the morning, the discovery of a forgotten book to absorb the mind or the sound of a hen happily announcing the laying of an egg in the comfort of her new nest in the stable.

There would have been no school for children in the past on days such as these. The teachers in Highland schools could assess the risks involved for children travelling even comparatively short distances from their homes and were given leave by the desk-bound authorities to close school early or to close it altogether on the worst days. The parents knew this and reacted accordingly.

At last, however, winter slackened its grip. The air had a whiff of fresh earth and the time for journeying had come. On a morning filled with early lark-song we set off, Helen and I, on the way to school. Her

Helen on the way to her first school

bag held only an apple and a pencil or two, but it was a much-prized piece of equipment. Bertha met us at the burn and we walked on cheerfully together. Half-way along the top road, at a junction with another smaller one, we stopped.

'See that stone' Bertha said, pointing to a flat boulder by the wayside. 'If the kids from along there have passed already they'll have put three small stones on the top of it. They haven't, so we'll put our two to show we've passed'. This was an intriguing idea and added a touch of excitement to the journey.

As we came in sight of the school three small girls came running to meet us—sisters, obviously, for they were as like as three apples on a tree. Smiling happily, they took charge of the new pupil and shepherded her inside. There was hardly time to wave goodbye. The feeling of calm confidence was very satisfactory. I remembered my own sickening trepidation on the first ever day of school and was very glad there was to be none of that. I waited a short while, had a welcome cup of tea with Mrs Maclean's daughter, who lived near the school, then set off to retrace my route.

It was a route we were to get to know well, in all kinds of weather. I thought of yesterday's children who had gone this way, many of them barefoot and without weather-proof coats. The rest of the day passed quickly and by late afternoon we began looking for the wandering scholars. The spring sky was beginning to fade when we glimpsed the two figures jumping the stepping-stones. A mutual wave of the hand and they moved their separate ways. The smaller figure seemed minute in the vast landscape, but she was coming steadily and surely home.

'How was school?'

'Fine.'

'Hungry?'

'A wee bit. Mrs Maclean gave me a scone.'

That was the first of many journeys made pleasurable by the kindly friendship and support of our neighbours. Mrs Maclean's always cheerful greeting and her farewell 'haste ye back' as she waved goodbye from the doorstep had made our day many a time. Often, in winter, she would have us in to sit at the fire burning in her old black range. Over tea and a scone straight from the oven, after making sure we were warm and dry, she would gaze through the bars at the glowing peats. With a small, contented half-smile she would say: 'Aye, we have much to be thankful for.' Then, a reminiscence, perhaps about the installation of the range and how it was a great advance on the days of the open fire, when the pot hung down the chimney and was used for baking 'oven'scones. Oatcakes were made on the girdle, then toasted in front of the fire.

In summer there would be crowdie and blackcurrant jam on the oatcake or scone and we would join Mrs Maclean on her little seat at the end of the house, where she could gaze up to the hills and the path to the 'glen', as Glen Urquhart was always known. This was the way the women of the glen took when they went to the battlefield at Culloden to look for their men. Still just discernible, in a fold of the high ground, is the remains of a croft house. 'That was the home of my dearest friend' she tells us. 'I mind when she had her first baby up there and the doctor came over on his horse from the glen'.

There was no question of loneliness in those days. No place, however remote, was beyond the reach of neighbours. You looked for the smoke rising from the chimney in the morning, the glow of the lamp in the window at night, and knew all was well. She was still remembering. 'There were shielings up there, so they had good company in the summer. That's when they took the cattle up to the high places to graze. The women and the girls stayed up there in wee huts and made butter and cheese when there was plenty milk. The men and boys stayed at home to watch the crops and maybe to put a new thatch on

Mrs Maclean

the roof of the house.

'What about school? Well, no book-learning, maybe, but I think they learned a lot...about animals and birds and flowers...You see that wee island in the burn there? It's called the 'island of the cheeses' because one day a sudden summer storm came up and washed the cheeses downstream, till they stuck there.'

The whole picture of summer life came clearly before our eyes. Many times we listened, enthralled, to these tales of the not-too-distant past. Most were happy, some had, perforce, to touch on the macabre, like the fact that, in a desperate attempt to cure epilepsy in a much-loved child, recourse was had to the burying of a live cockerel under the doorstep of the house. This was oral history in a very real sense. Remembering, now, I often wish we had had a tape-recorder in those days, though we might not have had the opportunity to use it much, as our time was mostly taken up with work of one kind or another. Listening to our neighbour was the happiest form of relaxation.

Mrs Maclean's husband was a skilled slater. He had roofed many houses in the neighbourhood, including our own, as thatch and corrugated iron gave way to slate. He was a reader, too, and was often to be found with a tome from the library. And he was a piper. It's said he liked to have a blow sitting astride a roof he had just finished slating! He kept the local Home Guard on the march during the war. It's sad indeed when folk like these neighbours of ours are no more. They taught us so much.

Helen's schooling went happily ahead. School was really an extension of home. With a teacher who was herself the mother of four growing children and whose classes numbered only a handful of pupils, it could hardly be otherwise. Each child was known as an individual and his or her background understood, so that needs could be met. There were many homely customs. On days of rain, wet shoes or coats would be put to dry by the glowing stove, which would be opened up for a few minutes so that numbed fingers could be warmed.

School for the junior classes finished at three. Any little ones living in the Caiplich area were allowed to wait in the schoolhouse till the big ones had finished, so that they could share a lift on the school bus which took the pupils from the nearby Junior Secondary up the road as far as the stile. Sometimes, on a day of sudden storm, by tea-time the burn, which had been easily crossed in the morning, was quite impassable. Then, our two would have to go up-country to the point where the road-bridge crossed the water. We'd watch for them, tracing their way along the moor, then we'd go to meet them so that Bertha could make for home. Our torches, in the dusk, would reveal two laughing faces, gleaming in the rain, with no hint of distress. On evenings in early summer they would take their time on the homeward way, looking for tiny trout in the clear brown water, watching the baby mallard ducklings trailing their mother through the rushes. These adventures were part of the school day.

Time spent in school was an adventure, too. Some of the younger pupils, having had their lesson and finished the task set them by the teacher, would listen in to the older ones' lesson. Information thus acquired surreptitiously had the gloss of magic about it, so that even the choice between 'should' and 'would' or the correct placing of the apostrophe seemed more like an intriguing puzzle than a dismal obligation.

The education in these small Highland schools at the time laid great emphasis on plain learning. It recognised the fact that most young minds are ready and eager to be stretched, to receive knowledge, to cope with facts, to find them fascinating. The patient guidance of dedicated teachers was always at hand, with quiet encouragement. Of course, there were problem children. They were coped with and accepted as they were at home, in their own family circle. And there were the fostered ones. Fostering had always been a part of Highland life. In older times the chief would foster a son in the home of a clansman, so that he grew up as part of the clan, in its widest sense as an extended family.

From very early centuries respect for learning had been widespread among the people. It was recognised that knowledge could have a direct bearing on the quality of daily living. Years of quiet observation by thoughtful men and women had led to the acquisition of knowledge about the value of plants as food sources or healing agents, about the ways of animals and insects, about the portents of wind or cloud. Those who had access to this continually increasing stock of knowledge would share what they knew with those around them and so became the first highly regarded teachers. They also had the status that doctors of medicine were later to enjoy, as their healing powers were recognised.

Spiritual needs were also catered for, as the stone monuments and burial mounds testify. So the three mainstays of Highland life—the teacher, the doctor and the minister of religion—had been established since the earliest times. We were fortunate in our first days here to have the dedicated teachers of the two local schools, a doctor in the next glen—son of the doctor who would take a short cut to see his patients, coming on horseback through the hills—and a minister of religion from the Islands who could conduct a service in the village hall and converse with his parishioners in Gaelic or English, as required.

Though plain learning was the order of the day in school—the 'Three Rs' had always been the basis of what was really a 'national curriculum'—importance was attached to the development of many skills. Singing had always been a part of Highland life. There were songs to go with every kind of work, love songs, dirges, lullabies. Singing came naturally to the children and was easily adapted into choral modes. Bible study and the learning of psalms and the catechism made a normal part of class work. The minister visited regularly. In older times, of course, the Presbytery ran the schools and kept a close eye on them. Religion was not for Sundays only, an attitude which surely made sense. There were lessons in drawing. The girls did needlework. Each had her own 'lap-bag', to keep her sewing or knitting in. These crafts, learnt at an early age, stood many of them in good stead in later life. The boys did many kinds of handicraft, skills which they could turn to good account later when they grew up to be 'do-it-yourself' men.

A kindly district nurse visited the school regularly and the services of doctor or dentist could be called on when needed. In this way the children soon lost their fear of medical examination. And what of playtime? The morning interval was short but the 'dinner-play' was longer.

These times were filled with energetic ball games, skipping games, round games, using the old traditional words with their meaning lost in time:

> The wind and the wind and the wind blows high,
> We are all maidens and we must all die...

This was sung quite calmly, with happily tripping steps. It is recognised today that these 'round' games represented a kind of therapy, curbing agressive instincts and encouraging co-operation. They have none of the over-competitiveness of many modern games and sporting activities. Even a 'counting-out' game—'ittle, ottle, blue bottle, ittle, ottle, out...' had its significance, leading to acceptance of the fact that chance has a hand in determining one's place in the order of things.

For the boys it was mostly a question of shinty practice. This was a game engaged in by players and spectators with as much enthusiasm, even passion, as football is today. The big, round ball was kicked about too, but it was the wee fellow, bashed by those wicked sticks, that took skill and strength to put between the posts, that was the favourite. In quieter moments the boys manipulated the 'bools'. Several of these, made of light brown clay, not as glamorous as their modern equivalents, I have retrieved from corners of the playground. Breaks in the school day, those short spells of play, were avidly enjoyed, especially because, before and after school, chores would be waiting.

So the summer term went by, with its easy walks to school, lessons in the garden on really warm days, long evenings outdoors at home, ball games and skipping games learnt with friends, running and jumping practice for Sports Day and at the end a book gifted to acknowledge progress.

Chapter
Three

On the worst days of rainstorm we would start up the old Hillman, an appropriate name for our ramshackle car, and go the long way round to school, picking up the other children on the way. This journey was usually made to the accompaniment of song, anything from opera to pop, from 'The Volga Boatmen', to 'Puppet on a String'. We were sure the kindly bus driver would take our two round to the bridge on the way home, knowing that the burn would be impassable.

Occasionally, snow, piled into drifts on the top stretch, would make the journey impossible. The bus driver would attempt it. Failing, he would report back to both schools, so that there was no concern for the children.

Then it was back to indoor pursuits again, to reading and to radio. The radio programmes for schools were quite invaluable. The act of listening could, in itself, lead to a lifelong ability to concentrate. It also built up the power of the imagination, as pictures in the mind grow out of the words and sound in the air waves. There was no question of leaving the radio on, to churn out an endless session of 'pop'. Weather forecasts, of course, were vitally important and were listened to in strict silence. News bulletins, too, were treated with respect. Though we lived at a remove from most of the events recorded, we had no wish to exclude the reality of happenings elsewhere. Atomic warfare, talk of the 'ultimate weapon', the exploration of outer space, mention of these and many other things came out of the air. It all had to be considered, since it could not be ignored, though it sometimes sounded like a nightmare from which we struggled to wake. Was reality, we wondered, not actually here, in our days of tending cattle and sheep, ducks and chickens and our beloved horse, of watching things grow and ripen, of battling with storms, of relishing sun and gentle rain? We believed it was. And we cherished the company of neighbours whose outlook was like ours. 'What will they come up with next?' was a common rhetorical question as we gathered for a ceilidh, after hearing

11

of the latest invention for exterminating half, at least, of the human race. Our agricultural experts were urging us to use chemical fertilisers on our 'marginal' fields. But these 'artificials', as they were known to our neighbours, were only grudgingly accepted as essential to the growing of good crops. As long as there were cattle, housed in winter, there was dung, and nothing, they reckoned, could beat dung for the production of full-bodied oats and tatties the size of neeps. How right they were, and how famished the land is without the sustenance of dung. Today, some kinds of dung can be bought, sanitised, in plastic bags. 'Back to basics' has become a slogan.

Coming home from one of these ceilidhs, on a calm winter evening, when frost had settled on the snowfields, we were quite overwhelmed by the crowding of the stars. They were enormous and seemingly so near you could stretch out a hand and pull one down to earth. Slowly, we picked out their names—Orion, the Seven Sisters, Venus, Jupiter, the Pole Star. We remembered the stories the old shepherds had invented for these stars, as they lay out in the desert watching their flocks. We concocted a home-made telescope. Many evenings after that we ventured out, muffled to the ears, to scan the Milky Way, to watch for shooting stars. Helen was enthralled. The world up there was mapped for our delight, adding another magic element to life. We composed a letter to the Astronomer Royal and got a most courteous reply, appreciating our interest and telling us what phenomena to look out for in our particular part of the country. Lately, a keen amateur astronomer has said he would dearly like to see an observatory set up here for the study of the skies.

With the coming of spring and regular days of schooling, evenings were spent mostly outside, watching the young stock: day-old chicks that had travelled miles from their place of birth and were to be installed beside their brooder-lamp, twin kids that their half-wild mother allowed us to glimpse from a safe distance and, of course, black-faced lambs everywhere. Helen, who had long been used to bringing in the cow for milking, was now promoted to feeding her calf from a pail, a job she enjoyed. She also had collie pups to feed and a pet lamb on a bottle, the little creature becoming importunate in its constant demand for sustenance, following us all over the house, sometimes bleating piteously from the landing upstairs.

It was a busy time but in the few spare hours we could carve out Helen was inspired to make herself a garden—just small plantings in a little patch of rock and heather, a natural rock garden. The sheep tended to ignore it as long as there was succulence for them elsewhere and it flourished quite happily. Meanwhile I was tending vegetables in a small plot fenced off in a corner of the near field. In older times every croft had a garden, just a patch guarded from marauding beasts by a solid, dry-stone wall. This wall sheltered the crops as no wire can. Kale, cabbage, carrots and onions would flourish happily, also blackcurrants and gooseberries. Turnips and potatoes would be grown on a field scale. Latterly, with the coming of the weekly food van, there was less incentive to grow the ingredients for broth, expecially when, some years, the crops were devastated by hungry roe-deer, which could leap five feet in the air! These little plots are still to be seen and they made excellent cover for ewes at lambing-time. Some crofters' wives, not to be outdone, grew little strips of pansies and wallflowers near the house, protected by some precious netting. Geraniums, of course, blazed in every window.

Summer came and holidays from school. When the peats were cut and drying and if the hay was in or safely standing and long before the corn was ready, we would think—'could we get away, just for a week-end?' Billy, from our neighbour's house, would come quite willingly to look after things for a short while.

Where to go was never questioned, or how. We simply packed a box of provisions, sleeping bags, a pot and a kettle and made for the west coast in the old Hillman. We slept in the van, cooked on the beach and revelled in the sea and on the sand. Many crofts in the west were still being worked at that time. Holiday homes were few and traffic was very light. The roads were narrow and twisting, with grass growing in the middle. We loved it that way! There were birds every-where, different birds, and different kinds of flowers—yellow irises and purple loosestrife along the roadside, corn marigolds in the little fields of oats. The working of the land in the traditional way was more environmentally friendly than it is with modern methods. Sea-weed was the main source of fertiliser and the crops were harvested from the edges inwards, instead of across. In this way creatures were safe-guarded. Nowadays, crofters in the west are being encouraged and subsidised to revert to these traditional ways in order to save en-dangered species, such as the corncrake. When spending a few days in North Uist recently I saw fields fertilised and cropped in this way. Oats and barley were flourishing and there was room for the mari-golds and tiny wild pansies. I heard—and even saw (an unusual event!)—a corncrake. We would return after a few days inspired and refreshed and ready to tackle the main harvests of the year—the oats and the tatties.

Before the days closed in, and whenever croft work allowed, Helen and I would go down, on a Saturday afternoon, to the village hall, where there was an ancient piano. We would get the key from the caretaker and I would show her what I knew of piano-playing, a few simple exercises and scales and how to read music. Then we would find a friend who lived nearby ready to regale us with tea, milk from her tiny Dexter cow, and all the news from her end of the parish, and we would swop magazines and newspapers. This outing put a highlight on the week.

Neighbourly visits were a much-prized facet of life. A child was greeted with as much grave courtesy as an adult, a gesture which inspired responsible behaviour. To know that you were assured of a welcome at any time was a great source of reassurance. No matter how busy your neighbour might be, work would be put aside till you were welcomed, news exchanged, and problems discussed, over a cup of tea or a dram. As lives were lived mostly to the same pattern difficulties were easily understood and could often be anticipated or even solved. Today, of course, neighbours live lives that differ outwardly, and though the fundamentals remain the same, problems cannot be shared or removed to the same extent.

Chapter Four

We were now reaching a sort of turning-point in our life on the croft. So far there was little return on our capital outlay in stock, implements and so on. Like so many crofters before us we realised that we would have to seek supplementary sources of income. Jim could get temporary work, but it would mean absence from home for certain spells. I could cope with the day-to-day running of the place as long as he was there at ploughing and harvest. We knew we could always rely on the help of neighbours in any time of crisis. We drew up a plan of campaign and discussed all the issues. One serious problem was the daily walk to school. With only myself on hand it would mean a chunk taken out of the morning hours. I had the cattle to see to, the horse and the poultry. The sheep could be left mostly to their own devices.

It was decided that, from the start of the next session, Helen would go to the Abriachan school, which was easier of access. There were few pupils, still mostly boys, but Helen was now well used to school and undaunted by the idea of change. We went to see the teacher. She belonged to Abriachan, and was an ex-pupil of the school and had taught in it from an early age. Her sister was an accomplished cook whose school dinners were famous. They both made us very welcome in the schoolhouse and said they would be happy to have Helen in school. We sat at the fire in the cosy kitchen, drank tea and ate fresh scones. They showed us how they, too, were making a rockery and gave us plants for Helen's garden.

Their friendly approach reassured us. Again, there was the feeling that school was just an extension of home, not an alien environment. It was good, we felt, to have a teacher whose family had been part of the community for generations. Her particular branch of it came from a croft not far from our own, on the high ground up the road. She and her sisters had been brought up to crofting life, so knew at first hand what problems the children had to face—doing jobs before and after school, getting out on days of storm, having to work long hours at harvest times, when home lessons should have been learnt.

One day in the summer holidays, before the change of school, when the first weeks of freedom and play had passed, I found Helen scrabbling about among the books, as I remembered doing at her age. There were many of my favourite French authors among them, some of my old French textbooks. These she found intriguing and an inspiration to learn the language. I thought of my mother and how she had set me off on my way to Paris, Grenoble, Provence. On our next trip to town I managed to unearth, from the bowels of our excellent bookshop, an attractive first book for very young beginners in the learning of French. Thereafter I made a good forty minutes available, every morning between early chores and midday mealtime, for explaining the elements of the language. Soon we were able to enjoy it, with songs and rhymes and little phrases, just as I had done those years ago.

Helen was well used to being set tasks to do on her own by the teacher in school and was quite happy for me to leave her with some simple exercises to work out. One day, when she had been a long time up in the bedroom where we worked, I went back to find her valiantly struggling to translate a story into English, looking up each word in a dictionary she'd found. We had to get a move on after that! She loved to pass on the songs and poems she'd learnt to friends who'd come to play. She had also acquired a smattering of Gaelic from Mrs Maclean, so the concept of language was one she could easily grasp.

'Ça va?'—'Ciamar a tha thu?'

The sounds went echoing happily round the house.

'Très bien, merci'—'Tha gu math tapadh leibh'.

It was sad to see the 'Language of Eden' dying out all around. In the houses of our neighbours middle-aged parents and foster-parents would communicate with each other in Gaelic, while the young generation spoke and understood, apart from a few phrases, only English. With the best of intentions the elders discouraged the use of the native tongue, knowing that work in the wider world where the young would have to go demanded the use of English. Teaching in the schools had long been conducted, compulsorily, in the official language of the State. In former times the use of Gaelic, or 'Erse', as it was known, identified the speaker as one of what was looked on as an alien people, a wild people who indulged in idolatry and even witchcraft.

Various attempts had been made to stamp out the use of this language. In 1609 some of the most powerful Highland clan chiefs were 'kidnapped' by the forces of the Crown, taken to the island of Iona and made to sign what became known as the 'Statutes of Iona'. They

Abriachan School and Schoolhouse

had to swear allegiance to the Crown, of course, and one of the Statutes, to which they had to put their name, stated that: 'Every gentleman or yeoman within the said Islandis or anyone having thriescor kye sall put at leist thair eldest sone, or having no children maill their eldest docter to the scuilles in the lowlnd and bring them up thair until they be found sufficientlie to speik, reid and write Inglishe.' This whole affair, was, of course, really an attempt to destroy the power of the Highland chiefs by destroying their culture, and was the start of a long process.

A hundred years later the Scottish Society for the Propagation of Christian Knowledge sought to enforce the use of English in the teaching in schools for the whole populace. In a school in the 'Glen' any pupil caught using the vernacular was punished severely. It is recorded that the master would hand a small piece of wood, called a 'tessera', to the first miscreant, who would then pass it on to the next and so on till the end of the day, when the punishments would be meted out. These were mostly devices to humiliate, the sinner being spat upon, put in a corner of the room or made to wear a collar of thorns.

Later, the prohibition of the vernacular was modified, as the children, who spoke only Gaelic at home, had become completely confused and were merely repeating sounds heard in school without any understanding. Today, strenuous efforts are being made to reinstate the Gaelic language, with the main teaching in some schools being in that language.

New literature is being created, poetry and prose of the finest quality. Some jobs in the Western Isles now demand a knowledge of Gaelic as part of the applicant's qualifications. Changed days!

When the new term began, in mid-August, Helen set off quite confidently on the new road to the new school. It was an easy way—up the field, over another stile, through the patch of felled woodland and the road was reached. Then it was a saunter or a race, with two or three others from a nearby house, down to the school, half a mile away.

Fears for safety on this road were few. It was a very little school now. The teacher herself must have felt it strange to be teaching a handful of children in one of the smaller rooms, when she had been one of nearly a hundred and taught by the master in the 'big' room. Many were the tales of his authoritarian rule! She had survived it and become a pupil-teacher before eventually returning as assistant and then head.

With so few children in front of her she was able to give them individual attention and tuition. Her sister saw to it that they were well fed, with good hot meals prepared in a kitchen which had been specially built a few years previously. An extra classroom had been built on as well, with facilities for the teaching of technical subjects for the boys and domestic science—now 'Home Economics'—for the girls. The purpose was to make the school into what was then known as a 'Junior Secondary', so that the children would not have to travel to Inverness to complete their education. But the school roll had been falling. This was due mostly to the fact that, as potential foster-parents were ageing, there were fewer and fewer fostered children in the area. It was they who had kept the intake of pupils to a reasonable level. Local children had grown up, and gone to raise families elsewhere. The croft could not support more than, perhaps, two, the older of whom would expect to inherit the tenancy or the freehold.

Schooling for Helen went on well enough, though the small numbers limited certain activities and the scope for play was also restricted. One memorable winter the children were at home almost as many days as they were in school, though they had only a short distance to go and most of it on a surfaced road. This was the winter of the 'big snow', when drifts froze into gigantic mounds of all shapes and sizes that nothing could shift. Blizzards blew up out of every airt. For weeks on end no wheeled vehicle could reach us. We learned to survive on eggs and tatties and oaten scones. Oatmeal sustains the brain, as is being rediscovered today. We certainly kept ours alive, with pencil and paper ploys, reading and the never-failing radio. Talks, music, drama, everything that came out of that small box of tricks added to the fabric of life and kept us in touch with worlds everywhere. It was certainly not a winter of discontent.

It was followed by an equally memorable summer. Eventually, of course, this meant a water shortage. The well dried almost to vanishing point. I took the washing to the burn. We even managed to bath in a pool still deep enough to sit in and well screened by bushes and dwarf alder! A swim in the loch, followed by a picnic tea among the meadowsweet and bog myrtle was a treat indulged in several times a week. We were always reluctant to leave the water. Dragonflies shimmered over the smooth surface. Swifts circled and screamed in the bright air overhead. Was this a taste of paradise?

We would go wading in again, watching the small fish darting in the shallows. This glorious warmth, after the long weeks of intense cold, had made us acutely aware of our dependence on the elements. Earth, air, fire, water—we saluted them as old friends, old friends to be treated with respect and a touch of awe. We felt linked, too, to the long-vanished people who had lived their lives out here, in the same landscape, thrilled, as we were, to hear the first lark in spring, happy with the wild harvests of autumn, biding their time in the cold months, keeping to the shelter of home. It is thought that the small island in the loch, where the black-headed gulls now nest, was originally a crannog, a man-made island, built as a safe dwelling-place for people and their livestock. So far, this has not been proven.

When at last the rain came, the well overflowed again and the water-butts were brimming. That was a signal for celebration, as we splashed about the steading in plastic macs and hats and wellingtons. Eyes shone out of bronzed faces as we licked the drops trickling from cheeks and brows!

Chapter
Five

Almost every Sunday, most of the year, we would go walking to explore different parts of our surroundings. Quite often we would go across a nearby slope of moorland, on our way to a higher point, where there was a wide encompassing view in all directions. One spring this heather-covered slope was burned, as part of a 'muir-burn' operation. This particular burning got out of hand and was excessively heavy. It uncovered what looked like the outlines of an old settlement. In the long beams of evening sunlight the shapes of hut circles and of small stone walls were clearly delineated, as on a three-dimensional map. Many times, after that, we walked it, always discovering new things—signs of terracing, of a larger, almost rectangular enclosure. Surely not a school! We dubbed it the village hall.

We visualised the children who must have lived there. Education, for them, would have meant learning the skills necessary for survival. We had often unearthed evidence of the long past efforts to keep fed and warm. Flint arrowheads, meticulously shaped, still lie at a spade's depth below the ground, though the wooden shafts have long since perished. Many a small boy must have watched, in fascination, as his father worked at the shaping. Soon he would have learnt the craft for himself, been on the alert to fit arrow to bow and take aim. Prey would have been plentiful—roe-deer, boar, wolf, grouse and waterfowl on the loch. The girls would have learnt to use another of the tools in my growing collection—the flint scraper. The skins of the animals brought in from the hunt would have been cleared of adhering body tissue before being dried, stretched and made into warm clothing.

Having learnt the techniques for survival from an early age, the children would have been proud to be part of the family work force, using their skills, as their counterparts do in Africa today. They would have had time and freedom for fun, too, time to wander up the hills, to paddle in the burns, to guddle small trout, to gather nuts and berries and honey from wild bees. Their imaginations would have been fired by the tales of heroes, of heroic beasts and of heroic men. Each tree and flower would have had a significance as healer or as food and a story telling of its origin and power. The world must have seemed a fairly magical place in spite of the hardships of daily life. Only now are we trying to get our children of today back in touch with the realities of physical hardship, of hunger and cold, as we send them off on 'adventure' trips and they struggle to find their way through storms and darkness on forays into the hills. And we're telling them stories again, great powerful stories of yesterday and today. Held in the spell of the story-teller's voice, their minds create the images they see.

The more we explored 'our' settlement the more determined we became to have it recognised by some acknowledged expert in the field of archaeology. We invited several likely people up to walk it with us—a retired schoolmaster, a countryside Ranger—till finally some experts from Edinburgh heard about it and it was duly and officially recognised as a settlement of late bronze or early iron age. It is now scheduled and known as the 'Loch Laide Settlement' or an early iron age farming settlement.

A photograph of the site is on display now, in the Inverness museum. Children have come to look at it as part of a summer activity known as 'Landscape Detection'. People walked it lately on an 'Archaeology Week' outing. The place was part of a Forestry Commission holding and has recently been sold to a private owner. He is, I'm glad to say, happy to have it identified, with a small plaque on a piece of natural stone. This will replace the sign put up some years ago by the Field Club, which had fallen into disrepair under the onslaught of weather. We hope that one day some of the hut sites may be excavated, so that more precise dating of the likely occupation can be established.

Meantime, it's good to know that people have lived here over so long a period of time, most leaving little trace—a few scattered stones, some patches of bright green among the heather, here and there a well, the outline of a hearth. It's a place that would have been attractive to settlers, even temporary ones, in nomadic times, then to their farming descendants. Not far away there is a cup-marked stone, mysterious sign, perhaps, of awareness of powers beyond their ken, perhaps of a signal to those powers. Who knows? It's good that they've left us with a mystery, in our world where we insist on explanations.

Living here, at 800 feet above sea level, with no dense afforestation such as that in lower regions, they would have had little likelihood of attack by predators, bear or wolf. Any human enemy could be spotted

A selection of crofting tools: home-made turnip chopper, flail and potato basket

from afar. The nearby loch would have been a source of food, along with small game, nuts and berries. There were scattered stands of birch, willow and alder, heather, scrub and stone, everything needed for the spare and daunted lives that were lived here over the millenia.

There were several deaths of elderly people in the neighbourhood about this time. We were privileged to help at some sad funerals, sad because they marked the end of an era. We went, later, to some displenishing sales and acquired, also sadly enough, some tools and plenishings—a peat spade, a cheese press, an iron pot—things which symbolised a way of life which was passing away, as the men and women who had lived it were passing away. This was a natural enough form of depopulation, but it meant that, as the younger family members had mostly moved away there was little chance of more children finding foster-homes in the neighbourhood. As the remaining boys in the school went on to secondary education, just two girls were left. This meant they got individual tuition and made good enough progress. But clearly there were limitations, a certain lack of stimulation and scope for practising social skills.

Then, one day in early spring, I glimpsed someone coming down through the felled woodland. It was a man, wearing a town suit and carrying a briefcase. He climbed the stile and made his way down the field. Who could it be? The house was in a mess. We had been at spring work in the fields, my hands were mud-stained, my skirt and jumper holed and crumpled. There was no time for repairs. Approaching the door, the visitor smiled and held out a hand in greeting. I grasped it, apologising for the mud. He laughed.

'Don't worry' he said, ' I know it's a busy time. I'm from the education department. I've come to tell you...we shall have to close the school. You'll understand...with two pupils...it's a question of economics.'

'Yes, of course, I understand. I thought, perhaps, as they're so near finishing their primary days...?'

'We might have delayed the closure another year or two. Alas, I'm afraid not.'

'So where...'

'...will the two girls go?'

'Yes.'

'They'll go to the primary department of the school over the back. In Kiltarlity. There will be transport. The bus will come to a point at the end of your place. To the west.'

This was near the bridge, where the driver used to drop them on days of storm, when they came home from Glenconvinth.

'I see. And this will start...'

'Next session. In August.'

'I see. Well...Thank you for letting us know.'

'It's a good school. And I daresay the girls will enjoy being among more children.'

'Well...will you...have a cup of tea?'

'Thank you. But I won't stop. I have to see the foster-parents of the other pupil. You will want time to think this over. Be sure to let me know if you have any queries. Now, I'll say goodbye.'

'Goodbye.'

I watched him go. I was thankful, in a way, that he didn't stay for the customary cup of tea. The kitchen was in a mess and it would have taken many minutes to get the dirt from under my fingernails. Besides, I needed time, as he had said, to think the situation through. The closing was inevitable, of course, and we must have known, even subconsciously, that it was coming.

To close a school...that must be a hard decision to have to make. In the case of Abriachan school there was clearly no alternative. With only two pupils on the roll it was costing as much to educate them as to send a boy to Eton or Harrow, so it was reckoned! But the closing of a school seems almost like sounding the death-knell of a district. A flourishing school brings people flocking in. And the name 'Abriachan',

THE LAST LESSON . . .

THE small country school at Glenconvinth, near Beauly, Inverness-shire, closes down tomorrow.

The 12 pupils are being transferred to Tomnacross School, two miles away. And headmaster Mr. Peter Macaskill (64) is retiring after 41 years in the Highlands.

He has been in the one-teacher school for 15 years. Before that he was headmaster at Dalwhinnie and at Northton, Harris.

"It is a sad moment for me," he said yesterday, "not only my retirement, but the closing of the school.

"When I arrived here there were about 60 pupils, but as people moved to the towns the number of children dwindled."

At the end of lessons tomorrow parents will climb the steep hill to the tree-shadowed school to say a thank you and farewell to the school and the schoolmaster.

The last day of teaching at Clenconvinth School, as described in the local paper. This was Helen's first school and the picture shows her first headmaster, Mr Peter Macaskill

as we will see later, had for years been synonymous with song, with Gaelic music and Gaelic song. That may be only a memory now, but good memories linger. They spread like the ripples on loch water in the wake of a delicate bird, till the singing rises again, in distant places, even on distant shores.

A few years after this the school at Glenconvinth was discontinued also. Some thirty years on there would be close on twenty children of primary school age in this area, a whole schoolful, with more to follow. It could not, of course, really have been foreseen that the place would become a favoured area for commuters, with their own transport, to live and bring up families. So transport was the answer for the few remaining scholars. School buses and mini-buses are everywhere, now. Their use, in some places, means early-morning departures and late home-comings, hard to endure in winter conditions of snow, frost or fog. Some children have home-sickness and bullying to contend with, also. Clearly, as the standard of facilities and equipment deemed essential in schools today is continually rising it would not be possible to bring all the old schools into line, so centralisation has to occur. There is the upkeep of the old buildings to be considered, too, the salaries of teachers, the provision of meals, and so on. Schooling is an essential social service. Yet it is a miss, in a community, not to see, and hear, the small bands of children on their way to and from school. It's a miss for the children, too, not walking the road, with a saunter and a last-minute rush to beat the bell in the morning and a great capering of freedom on the way home.

The girls took the news of their move to a new school quite calmly. The adaptability of the young has always amazed me. I think, as long as they have the security of a stable background, the outside world can wobble as it likes.

Chapter
Six

It may have wobbled a little for these two in their first days at this much bigger school, but I think children grow a light covering of protective skin, a sort of bullet-proof vest, strong enough to withstand the impact of any slight shafts that might be coming their way. There was now diversity of lessons and pupils and teachers, which was intriguing but not overwhelming. Everyone made our two from the wilds most welcome. New friendships were formed. One in particular, for Helen, was to be of real and lasting value. There were better facilities for the practice of more formal sporting activities. Hop-scotch and skipping were still enjoyed but now there was really competitive jumping and even hurdling.

In no time at all, it seemed, the famous '11 Plus' was over and a place at the Royal Academy in Inverness assured. This was a school renowned throughout the country. I remembered from my own student days in Edinburgh how highly regarded were the people from Inverness. Kingwall and Kingussie schools also produced students of the highest calibre, many of them coming from the Islands and the far west.

So, after a care-free summer—swimming, camping, reading sprawled on the grass—there was the first day at school number four and another big first—the first day as a weekly boarder at the school hostel in Inverness. This is a situation which many children in the Highlands, and especially the Islands, have to cope with. In some places—Benbecula, for instance, and Castlebay in Barra—big new schools have been built, offering a full secondary education and many community facilities—swimming-pool, library, restaurant and so on. Here the move is less drastic. Children have to board from Monday to Friday, but to come from, say Eriskay to Benbecula is not too traumatic. Those coming from the small, close-knit communities of the small isles to Dingwall, Inverness, even Kingussie, were often lonely and homesick for quite a time. And there were, of course, the sometimes doubtful distractions of town life for the uninitiated.

We had no car at this time and the daily walk to and from the bus on the main road would have been too much, even in summer. But this further adaptation to living with strangers during the week was accomplished easily enough. We met the bus in late afternoon on Friday and would walk down again on Sunday evening. The new subjects —maths and science—were again intriguing, though a little intimidating. Latin was a bit of a conundrum, with words that seemed to go their own strange ways. As we walked down to the bus in the autumn dusk I would rack my brains to remember case endings and declensions and we'd end up intoning '*rosa, rosa, rosam*' or '*amo, amas, amat*', as the roe-deer barked in greeting and an owl hooted encouragement. The house seemed empty and cheerless during the week, but we filled the days with work and relished the weekends.

I spent a good many hours trying to made a contribution to our supplementary income in the only way I knew—by writing. I had always, since childhood, had paper and pencil handy, for writing a diary, editing a junior magazine and so on. Poems, too, I had secreted at the back of a drawer. Now I settled down to writing about what I knew best—Highland life, Highland history. I had submitted a piece about a Highland Christmas to the BBC people in Aberdeen. To my amazement I got word from them that, as they would like me to read it myself, would I please give them a call on the telephone so that they could judge the suitability of my voice. We had no telephone. I walked down the road to the phone box and dialled the number indicated. Then—what to say? 'Anything at all', someone said at the other end. In a panic, I intoned: 'Mary had a little lamb, Its fleece was...'

A giggle came down the line. 'That's fine' the voice said. 'Can you be here at ten o'clock next Tuesday morning?'

'I...I think so. Yes. All right.'

'Good. See you then.'

So, somehow, the journey was arranged and accomplished. A lift to the station, train to Aberdeen, an overnight stay at the home of an old student friend and by 10 am the next morning I was in the studio. A warm welcome was reassuring, then came 'rehearsal', watching for the green light in the producer's loft, reading what seemed to sound like sheer nonsense from one's script, fitted in with other much more sensible-sounding items. Then—dispersal, with the injunction to be back in good time for the 'real thing', at 2 o'clock. I wandered the streets, desperately hoping for a huge hole to open, swallow me up and spare me the coming ordeal. But, alas, no cataclysm occurred. On the precise dot the green light came on and I was 'on the air'. After the first moments the panic, mercifully, subsided. I got to the end of my piece.

Then the journey back to normality. On arrival home the family outcry was 'Oh, what a pity...you were too nervous...you didn't read it!' 'What?' I screamed. 'Of course I read it. What do you mean?'

It transpired that my voice, over the air, had been unrecognisable to my nearest and dearest! The follow-up to the broadcast was quite gratifying. There were letters from Army wives in Germany and one I particularly treasured from Alasdair Alpin MacGregor, of Western Isles fame.

After that I did several short stories and documentaries for schools for the BBC. The stories—'Morning Stories'—were read from London by James McKechnie. With his Highland background he seemed really to enjoy what he was reading and he made an excellent job of the broadcasts. The producer, James Langham, showed great empathy and this collaboration went on for a number of years. For the documentaries I found another very co-operative producer, Marinell Ash, a history graduate of St Andrews. We worked happily together until her untimely death some years later. I was also contributing short pieces about crofting life to the *Scotsman* publications and a book about our own life on a croft had been accepted by Oliver and Boyd, the highly regarded Edinburgh firm. The stories and the pieces in the old *Weekly Scotsman* brought us letters and pen-friendships from many parts of the world, particularly America and Australia. The feel for the 'old' country dies hard.

This was satisfactory and rewarding but still the gap in income was not really filled. We had to decide, reluctantly, to give up working the croft, to sell the stock and to let the land for grazing. Finally, it was remembered that I had a degree in French, there was a demand for teachers and a Special Recruitment Scheme had been set up to encourage older people to go into teaching. Small grants were available to help with costs. So—Helen went to stay in a school friend's house, Jim found a lodging near his work and I went off to Aberdeen to take a six-month training course in the art and craft of teaching.

I adapted to the life of a 'mature' student more readily than I could have thought possible. After years of working on the croft—harvesting, lambing, butter-making, peat-cutting—it was certainly strange, first of all, just to be sitting down, listening to lectures, reading. The 'Master of Method' was a big, amazing man, a poet, whose endearing Aberdeenshire voice told of his country origins. He made a link with home. Strangely enough, he had read my newly-published book and liked it to the extent that he put ten copies of it into the College library. This gave me a real lift.

My fellow students, mostly just graduated from the University, were inclined not to take the training too seriously. For me it was essential. I had been out of touch for so long with scholastic matters. We had lectures in Method, psychology and some from a medical man who showed us how to recognise symptoms of epilepsy, dyslexia and other conditions. The only thing they couldn't really teach us was how to handle a class of reluctant pupils who were only waiting for the bell to ring. We did go out to schools and got a certain amount of practice, but we knew this was not exactly for 'real'.

My first assignment, after only a few weeks in the College, was to a Primary School. I was lucky to find there an excellent young teacher who made me very welcome and initiated me into the ways of marking the register, learning to fit names to faces, how to spread questions round the class, and so on. My College tutor came to 'hear' my first lesson. There was no French taught, so I had to take the class in history, on the subject of the battle of Bannockburn. The story of that battle has stayed in my mind ever since! Eventually I was sent to a secondary school and duly took a lesson in French in front of a Chief Inspector who happened to be visiting! By that time I was beginning to feel my way and did not find the occasion as much of an ordeal as I had feared.

I lodged in a small bed-sitting room, in a pleasant house, near the outskirts of the town, with kind and very understanding landladies. Most evenings I spent reading or writing the innumerable set essays, trying to shut out thoughts of life as I knew it. I treasured the regular hospitality of my friend from student days. The weekends, mostly, were the dreariest times. I would walk out into the flat countryside, visualising the hills and the wide sweeps of moorland that formed the usual background to my days. We kept in touch, the three of us, with many letters and phone calls. An occasional celebration brought us together for a Friday to Monday break, when the good ladies of the house provided accommodation. Christmas came and holidays. We opened up the house and had a brief good spell together. After that, with the daylight soon lengthening, time raced ahead. I passed the necessary exams, had an interview with the Director of Education for Inverness-shire, and found I had a job teaching French in the High School of Inverness.

We rented a small flat in the town and put our furniture, books, pictures, all our precious things, in store. Then, one day in late summer,

I set off for school. It was a glorious morning. My mind, still on automatic pilot, registered that it would be a great day for ripening the crops. I came back to earth. A great day for marking the register, assembling the class and getting into some sort of a stride. So it went on. I had the good fortune to have a genial and understanding headmaster and a head of department who quickly became a friend. Many people in other departments were most supportive, too.

Looking at the sea of young faces confronting me—in those days we had 40 plus in some classes—I wondered how I would ever get to know even their names, let alone what sort of people they were, how best to approach each one in the learning process. Sometimes I imagined how it must have been in the schoolroom at Abriachan—70 pupils facing you in tiered rows, all at different stages and many of them still thinking in Gaelic!

Eventually I found it much easier than I would have thought possible to attach names to faces. To fathom what went on in the heads behind the faces was a much more difficult task. Perhaps my biggest problem was learning to cope with a huge class of 'less able' boys who came to my room for 'Bible'. We were all expected to take classes in scripture, though few of us were qualified to do so. Eventually I learned a few tricks and found even the toughest customers quite liked listening to a Bible story, preferably one of the more bloodthirsty ones, and then, perhaps, drawing an illustration to it, in colour. With older boys I sometimes read stories of the missionaries in Africa or China and found they could relate to them. With all the classes I learned many tactics and often found surprising elements of kindly goodwill in the most unlikely sources. Any human predicament, which many of the children probably quite often experienced, always evoked a sympathetic response. Once, for instance, when I had to apologise for not having the homework corrected as my husband had had an accident and had to go into hospital, there were expressions of gloom on the faces and little moans of sympathy. Then, after the interval, the scruffiest little girl in the class slipped a tube of fruit drops on to my table as she passed. What did the correct agreement of the past participle really matter compared to these glimpses of humanity?

It was when starting work with a second year class that I encountered a real problem. We had got past the stage of naming objects, of repeating attractive little phrases, of reading and even writing some simple stories, of singing French folk songs and of learning something about France. Now, with pupils who would be expected to write a fairly well turned-out piece of prose in a couple of years' time, I was up against the fact that the teaching of grammar was fast disappearing from lessons in the English language. I remembered my early days in an old-established 'Grammar' school near Edinburgh, the only secondary school in place. It was so old that the classrooms were tiered and the blackboard stood on an easel. There, in our early teens, we read Virgil and Shakespeare and the *Canterbury Tales* and were introduced to Euclid. 'Grammar', by comparison, was almost a relaxing exercise, like solving a crossword puzzle. I remember analysis and parsing, parts of speech, subordinate clauses, figures of speech with their marvellous names, derivations and so on. We had some wonderful teachers and a lot of fun, addressing each other in Chaucerian English, with much ribald laughter. Now, with my 13-year-olds, the problem was how to explain the notion of tenses, of subject and object, of direct and indirect object, let alone of participles, to young minds devoid of any points of reference. To make the past participle agree with a preceding direct object is imperative when it comes to writing a letter to one's pen-pal with a description of holiday adventures. I didn't dare admit that sometimes the French themselves get this wrong! Slowly, with the discreet application of carrot (or meringue) and stick (very gentle) I would manage to get a few notions of grammar across. Some of the girls actually came to enjoy getting things right. But some boys decided that French was not for them, despite the fact it would come in handy for holidays abroad.

In those early teaching days I would come home at half past four, utterly exhausted, but with some small sense of achievement, and after a short stretch relaxing on the sofa and a family supper, I would tackle correcting a pile of jotters and be ready for next day. At the end of the month that pay cheque was certainly a welcome sight. The money was essential for our daily living. But as time went by the teaching itself, and the learning how to teach, became absorbing and more and more deeply rewarding.

I had been teaching for about a year when the gods flashed a smile at us. We were told that the schoolhouse, attached to the school at Abriachan, was available to rent, as the occupant, a teacher in Inverness, was leaving to take up another post. His wife had worked the Post Office from the front porch. We applied immediately for the tenancy. There was not a great demand for it as to many people Abriachan was a remote, almost inaccessible small spot on the map. For us, it was home. In actual fact, it is only ten miles from Inverness. The access road is steep, but there are several passing places and latterly crash barriers have been erected. It didn't daunt us. We knew it well. The rental of the house was minimal. Jim would do the Post Office.

But—I had to learn to drive. Being over-anxious to succeed, I failed the test several times. Then, at last, I managed to discard the 'L' plates and could sail quite happily up and down the hill, though reversing on the steeper gradients could be quite perilous in times of frost or snow. We had bought a small Austin van with collapsible rear seats. A normal, cushion-seated car was still not quite our style. The van had possibilities for picnicking and camping, as well as for the transport of equipment and goods. It proved all its possibilities over the years, taking us on camping holidays in many parts.

Chapter
Seven

We settled gradually into our new life in the Schoolhouse. Helen was preparing for exams at the Academy, I was acquiring some skill in the art of teaching, Jim was learning to deal with daily customers and the handling of stamps, postal orders, pensions and so on. Learning is a continuous process, we are told, a lifelong process, and so it was proving with us. Teachers of old, we had heard, quite often acted as Postmasters, in return for a small welcome addition to their pay. Deliveries were infrequent, perhaps twice a week in summer, seldom in winter. The bearer would come on foot or on horseback. Some lost their lives in flood or blizzard. In Abriachan, in later days, the steamer brought the mail from Inverness, the postie collecting it at the pier. Many a crofter receiving a letter, perhaps from a relative emigrated to America, would seek the schoolmaster's help in reading it and in composing a reply. This custom prevailed until quite recent times, not so much for the actual reading of the missive and writing the reply, but in the explaining of Government directives and the filling up of forms. This was a task we ourselves were to be glad to perform over the years.

Our first entry into the Schoolhouse, with a large key to the front door, was a memorable occasion. We had long known it from the outside, of course, having passed by many times, walking or on our way to town. It had often seemed to us like a minor mansion, standing in its own grounds, in the shelter of its huge cypresses and pines and hawthorn hedge. There were rhododendrons, too, the hallmark of the Highland estate. Was this really going to be our home? The sitting room faced south, big sash windows looking across grass and hedge to a hillside of heather and scattered trees. The bedroom above was an equally pleasant room. There were two further bedrooms, kitchen, scullery and bathroom. It was a typically Victorian house, with high ceilings, panelled doors each with brass handle and keyed lock, picture rails, moulded skirtings and fireplaces to match. It would have been built soon after the Education Act of 1872.

We visualised the various headmasters who had lived there, and their families. Some were remembered happily, we knew, others with feelings mixed with trepidation or awe. All had left their mark on the community. We were to learn much more about them in later days. For the time being we were spending the Easter holiday getting our furniture out of store, unpacking cherished books and pictures, settling in. It was a real spring. Bulbs were pushing through along the verges—snowdrops, crocuses, daffodils. Soon many self-sown early flowers were to appear. We explored the garden to the back. Here, the plots were largely over-grown. The short-term tenants who had latterly occupied the house had had young families and not the time to tackle the required cultivation. This task would have to wait till we ourselves had the opportunity to get round to it.

Meantime, we had finally and reluctantly decided we would have to sell the croft. A neighbouring crofter had for long been keen to acquire it. He worked it well, bringing in more rough ground, and it is still being worked, for which we are thankful. Our 'croft' now consisted of, perhaps, a quarter of an acre of ground, some of it tidy, some of it a wilderness. The tidy part was the typical Victorian frontage of grass, hedge, laurel, trees and one flower border. The walls of house and school were ivy-covered. The wilderness was at the back. Here, the ground sloped up to the heather-covered moor beyond and had been terraced into plots to be used for teaching gardening. Willowherb had taken over an area at the top, raspberries were growing wild, a few blackcurrant bushes had survived.

We heard stories of one headmaster who would have great fires of brushwood in the garden, to provide fertiliser for the vegetables. We liked this good organic thinking. He had certainly made a start at creating a garden out of a plot of ground and had got 'gardening' firmly on the curriculum. Another headmaster had installed stone drains and another, in later years, took the garden into another league, making a rockery, a herbaceous border, a lawn. This had subsequently to be planted with potatoes in the 'dig for victory' campaign during the Second World War. He also kept goats, chickens and bees and set a great example of self-sufficiency.

One spring, we decided it was time to make a start at bringing the place under control. With the lengthening daylight I would come home as early and as fast as possible so as to get in a couple of hours battling before supper. 'Battling' was really an appropriate verb. As well as the willowherb which was beginning to appear in its first delicate shoots, which look deceptively like asparagus, there were also chunky shoots of what turned out to be sweet cicely. A little of this would be a good thing, I knew, but the quantity of shoots that were appearing was quite overwhelming. I tried in vain to eradicate the roots. They were brown and enormous and seemed to go down to the centre of the earth. The hollow stems made excellent pea-shooters, we were told, and always brought back memories of schooldays to old pupils. I reminded myself that the flowers of this plant could be used as a sweetener when stewing fruit, and the old monks, God rest their souls, would concoct a liqueur from it. I now give a small plant to interested friends, with dire warnings to keep the thing in check.

We hired a rotavator and rough-cleared half of the plots in one day. The rest were to wait another year. Here and there we came on the stone drains that had been so carefully constructed long before the coming of mechanical cultivation. We tried desperately to avoid them and to repair any that had been damaged. We lit huge bonfires of burnable material and piled much debris into what became vast compost heaps. One or two boys in the neighbourhood, keen to earn a little pocket-money, gave a hand on a Saturday. We unearthed small stone paths, where the plots had been terraced. We cleared small rubbish dumps of broken glass and discarded plastic toys.

Against the wall at the top was a large mound covered in nettles, ground elder, thistles, dockens, growth of every kind. Nettles usually mean a dump of non-plastic interest. One day I stuck a spade in. It clashed against some obstruction. Another dig and I unearthed a small pile of old school slates. They must have been abandoned the day the jotters came in! Thereafter my helper and I dug and dug. We found some china inkwells and a cream jar, among many broken pieces of pottery and glass. The pottery fragments themselves, bits of old porridge bowls and plates, are very decorative. I use them to make small mosaic patterns among rock plants or in bowls of bulbs. They are beautifully coloured reminders of the old way of life. We eventually cleared almost the whole dump but found nothing more of real interest. People everywhere, at that time, were laboriously working over old rubbish dumps in the hope of finding treasure. The surrounds of one or two ruined mansions in the neighbourhood seemed promising, but must have been explored long since, for we found nothing but broken wine bottles. Our happiest hunting-ground was a village dump, not far away, where we came on a box of books, a huge earthenware crock and, unbelievably, a silver spoon!

About this time, we got permission from the Education Authority to house the small collection of crofting implements and artefacts we had brought with us in the outside classroom at the top of the playground.

Early days at the Crofting Museum

We whitewashed the walls and cleaned up the objects for display—the peat-spade, the hay-rake, the pitchfork, the scythe—things we had handled so many times when working the croft and which were rapidly going out of use. There were domestic artefacts to clean, too—a girdle, an iron kettle, a cheese press, a butter churn. We began to make a catalogue of the items, with short notes on their provenance and use. We would welcome anyone who cared to handle and examine them. To some people they were strange, almost unknown objects, to others they brought back memories and engendered fascinating tales of former times. This was our reward—to see the look on the face of the old man as he picked up the peat-spade, put his foot on the bracket and remembered the far-off days of May-time at the peats. There was the granny, too, who brought a grandchild to show her, in clear words, exactly how you made the butter, the cheese, the oatcakes and the scones.

The school itself, with its three classrooms and small cloakroom at the back, was still unknown territory to us. It had a quite separate front and back door, though it shared a roof with the house. It was being used by the Education Authority as a store to house surplus desks and benches and other school equipment. Occasionally a lorry would arrive to discharge a load or to take one away. The cooker was removed from the outside kitchen, leaving a very derelict small building.

One day in early summer I looked up from weeding the flower border I was making at the front of the house as I heard a strange sound I couldn't easily identify. It stopped. It came again. It was coming from the school, a gentle thudding against the inside of the window. I looked closely. Young starlings were trapped in there, trying desperately to make for the light, the air and freedom. Their parents had nested under the eaves and the young birds must have found their way into the loft and down through a ventilator into the schoolroom. We rang the Authorities asking for someone to open the place so as to release the birds. Next day an official travelled the ten miles, at our request, and thereafter we were given a key to the premises for keeps! We thanked the starlings!

So, at last, we were able to venture in on our own and take a long look at this ancient seat of learning. Its use as a store was to be discontinued, we were told. We were glad of that. It seemed an ignominious use for such a venerable old building.

The 'big' room, where the headmaster taught the senior classes, had originally been bigger than it is today, accommodating over a hundred children. One end had been partitioned off in later years to make a room for juniors, when an extra member of staff was appointed. There was a third room, known as the 'infants'. The big room had been tiered, so that the pupils at the back could see, and be seen by, the teacher. He would stand with his back to the open fire, keeping most of the heat from the children. Those at the top of the room spent many winter days with frozen fingers. There was an open fire in the infants' room, too. Here there would have been less 'talk and chalk', a little more movement allowed and better circulation of warmth! In the partitioned room, the only one used in later days, a stove had been installed, with an iron flue projecting through the wall. The desks used by the last pupils had gone, but the cupboard still held books—readers, history and geography and arithmetic books—and a box full of green and white shorts for wear on Sports Day. These things, evidently, were considered so far out of date as to be worthless. To us, they brought glimpses of the generation of children who had come here, some willingly, some unwillingly, to school.

We went into the big room again. A schoolroom empty of children is indeed a sad place. Looking closely round, we could visualise the rows of faces, the hands shooting up to please the teacher, with tentative proffered answers to his peremptory questioning, the undercover smirking that must have occurred when a harsh teacher was in command and his back was momentarily turned. We could hear the drone of repeated 'tables' and of the long drawn-out spelling of complicated words. The Shorter Catechism, question and answer, would be intoned. There would be singing, too, and sometimes in Gaelic, with a Gaelic-speaking teacher, and that would have been welcome, though knuckles would have been rapped if anyone hit a wrong note. Tales were often told of the standard of singing in the 1920s which had earned the school a reputation as almost a 'Sang' school, when cups and prizes were won in competitions and at the Mod.

On the wall by the door is a marker-board for recording the children's heights. The little orphans from Glasgow would have had a long way to go till they caught up with the crofters' children. We could see their small, startled faces on their first day in school, when they were weighed and measured and given their new identity.

Outside there are two playgrounds and a shelter divided in two—a girls' and a boys'. This shelter was built in the mid-twenties when the parents of children living two or three miles away petitioned for them to be allowed to use the classroom at dinner-time on stormy days. Many scrawled initials are clearly visible. J. McD. must surely have been a John Macdonald, or a James; D. C. could have been a Duncan Chisholm; D. F. for Donald Fraser...? The girls seem to have been less keen to leave a record of their presence.

Up at the top of the playground is a row of small 'privies', known in the older records as the 'offices', small closets with slats in the doors. Town children who see them today are scared to use them in case someone peers in! In their day they were a great advance on the old pail and spade!

I have the great good fortune to have as a neighbour a former pupil whose schooldays began in 1913. He remembers them well, happy times with a patient lady in the Infants' Room, times of trepidation in the 'big' room, where discipline had to be strict when 70 or more children, seated in 'galleries', as the tiered benches were known, had to be taught by the one teacher. The headmaster at that time was the first non-Gaelic speaker to be appointed. There were good times working the garden, good games of shinty and football in the playground or in the field over the road. And there were the holidays, with swimming in the loch in summer, and ferreting and going down to the pier to meet the steamer. In winter there was sledging, very precariously, on sheets of corrugated iron.

My neighbour's mother was among the early intake of pupils into this new post-1872 school and had happy memories of her days with a Highland master. She emerged as one of the few who could read and

An ex-pupil of the 'new' school (in 1913-18) standing by the remains of the 'old', Mr Lachlan's, school

write Gaelic, as well as use it in daily conversation. She also wrote verse, in the bardic tradition.

His father had been a pupil in the last days of the 'old' school, with a schoolmaster whose Gaelic was more fluent than his English. Both these Highland schoolmasters are remembered with affection. Sadly, my neighbour and his brothers and sisters were not encouraged to use their native tongue. English was needed in the wider world where job prospects were better. But the words of the old songs and the place-names of fields and hills and lochs are firmly rooted in their memories. Their great-uncle, who was descended from Helen McLachlan, daughter of an eighteenth-century schoolmaster, was known as the 'Bard', his poetic gift no doubt bequeathed by 'Mr Lachlan'.

As time went by we found ourselves wandering often into the school, admiring the workmanship of the building, the great blocks of red sandstone, the lofty ceilings, the window built high up the walls so that young minds were not distracted by the sight of the outside world.

A SCHOOL IN THE HILLS

The sandstone for the window surrounds was brought from a quarry down by Loch Ness. The walls are of local whinstone and granite, as so many of the houses are, built by masons who could hew and shape the stone as well as build it. The roof timbers would have been supplied by the estate and the slates would have come from Ballachulish. In the plans it is described as a 'school for 100 pupils'. It became almost as much part of our lives as the adjoining house we lived in.

Chapter
Eight

Abriachan is a surprising place. Less than ten miles after leaving Inverness, on a good tarmac road to the west, you turn off, rise quickly to 800 feet or so and are in a country of old croft land, heather and pine. Most of the heather has now been covered in rows of planted conifer, but those years ago, when the moors stretched for miles, it was the sweeps of heather which brought us a most interesting and inspiring summer.

One lovely morning a young man called Peter Watkins came to the door to tell us he was about to make a film of the battle of Culloden. 'Come in!' we said, opening the door wide in welcome. This sounded like something after our own hearts. He went on to explain that the actual site of the battle was not suitable for filming as trees had largely taken over the ground. (It has since been de-forested and restored to its former state.) He had got permission from the landowner to film on the Abriachan moors and the Education Authority had authorised the use of the old school as a base. He spoke with great clarity and enthusiasm and had obviously done much serious research. We assured him of our whole-hearted support.

Next day we stood wide-eyed on the doorstep to watch the arrival of actors and crew. They were to come out in buses, on a daily basis, already rigged out as Highlanders or Redcoats, to the delight and amazement of passing motorists and walkers. Rations were provided by a restaurant in Inverness. Cameras, microphones, all the filming gear and huge baskets of props were unloaded into the schoolroom, a cannon was parked in the playground shelter. Ponies from a nearby riding school had been hired. A band of 'extras', mostly young men from Inverness, was despatched up the hill to build the famous dry-stane dyke, which figured largely in the battle. This wall was to stand for many years, providing welcome shelter for sheep!

Then, it came time for the battle to start. One morning I went up to the moor. A group of young Highlanders was standing at the ready, broadswords swirling, targes held firm, obviously desperate to have a go at the line of Redcoats in the distance, well marshalled and equipped, standing in an orderly squad. Peter shouted 'Hold on! Remember you're dead beat. You've done a long march and had no sleep. You're starving. You've had no food for days. Some of you aren't sure what all this is about. I want to see all that in your faces. In the way you move. Right?'

Gradually Peter got across to the people in the film the reality of what they had to portray. They had to learn something of the background and the intricacies of the situation. There were split loyalties among the clans, jealousies and disagreements between the commanders of the Highland forces, the Prince obstinately refusing to allow his most able general, Lord George Murray, to make the most important decisions on the course of the fighting. The stark fact was that defeat for the Highland force was inevitable since the Government army consisted of 9,000 fighting men, well equipped and provisioned, with adequate cavalry and cannon, while the Highlanders numbered 5,000, all desperately ill-prepared and obliged to operate on ground unsuited to their traditional way of fighting.

We went up to watch the encounters on the moor, marvelling at the skill of the cameraman as no one was injured in the bursts of violent activity he had to capture on film. One day, in late afternoon, a dishevelled Redcoat appeared at the door, in a state of near collapse. We took him in, slipped off his tunic, administered a wee dram, then a cup of hot tea and some oatcake. 'Thanks' he murmured, smiling apologetically. 'Sorry about this. I died three times up there in the rain before I got it right.' We laughed. Peter was concerned. But there had to be perfection. That was the making of the film.

With the fighting ended we glimpsed the Prince, weary and unkempt, leaving the battlefield and the dead, making for the hills, followed by a few exhausted Highlanders. This is, I think, a fair picture of the man. He had shown courage when things were going his way, but vanity and obstinacy betrayed him in times of stress.

This film is a documentary, a film for our time. In the aftermath of the battle we find the real meaning of the whole suppression of the Jacobite cause. After two weeks filming on the moor, scenes were shot in the old streets of Inverness and in the dungeons of Fort George, showing the atrocious treatment of prisoners. Then, in the hills of Glencoe, the continuing barbarity of pillage, rape, the burning of houses, the butchering of whole families, the whole desperate effort to wipe out an ancient race, was portrayed. The aftermath was eventually to include the banning of traditional garb, the kilt, the tartan, the playing of the pipes, the carrying of weapons. Today we call this ethnic cleansing.

All this comes out in the film. Made on the tightest of budgets, with integrity, energy and imagination backed by careful research, as an indictment of war and barbarity it is superb.

As I write, this year, I have had the great pleasure of attending a reunion of people involved in the making of this great film. Thirty years on, Peter Watkins has still the look of youth which I remember. The cameraman is as active as ever. We watched a screening of the film, spell-bound. Then we talked and talked. Next day they came out to Abriachan, walked the battlefield and went into the old schoolroom. At once, more memories came back. 'That was where I changed my boots', 'The tea-urn steamed over there', 'Mmm...I remember...'

I hope this film will be seen and seen again. Will we ever learn? A showing once a year might help.

Our next encounter with film-makers was a few summers later when a truck-load of young students from a London Film School drew up in the playground. They had heard about the museum collection from a colleague in Inverness and wanted to borrow some items for a film they were making about the 'Seven Men of Glenmoriston' who hid the Prince, after Culloden, in a cave in the wilds of Glenmoriston. Though suffering great hardship and with their lives at risk, they stead-fastly refused to accept the price that was on the royal head. Strangely enough, as we told the students, a descendent of one of the 'Men' had lived at one time in Abriachan.

We lent them a creel, a whisky jar, some items of clothing and wished them well. Our two granddaughters, then small girls, on holi-day here at the time, were invited to take part in the film as extras. After a long day they came home, with blackened faces, exhausted and not too thrilled with film-making! The museum items were eventu-ally returned, a little the worse for wear, and we never heard what success the film achieved.

On another summer day, of the wet and windy kind, I looked up from some indoor chores to find a young woman nearing the door.

'We're making a film. We'd like some shots of open moor ground. We thought there would be some here. Could you tell us where we might go? Perhaps...some open moor and...some rough stone walling...'

'Yes. I think you could find that. Perhaps further up the road. I could show you...'

'Thanks. We're just going to have lunch. Then we'll follow your guidance.'

'Right.'

I went with her to the gate. A small fleet of vehicles was parked along the verge, among them a snack-bar. People of all shapes and ages, dressed in '20s country-worker style, were queuing for soup and pies. They were windblown and wet. I opened up the school to let them eat in comfort. They were making a film based on a story by Jessie Kesson.

'She lived here for a while, as a young girl. A few old people remember her. There's the house...up on the hill.'

They were interested, but busy eating and discussing film technique. I gave them directions to the moor ground and waved them off. Some years later I saw two or three seconds' worth of the moor ground in the film *Another Time, Another Place*, which won great acclaim.

Looking back on these encounters I think we must have been, unwittingly, pioneering the current trend of locating films in the Highland area. None of the recent ones have come up to the standard set by our early ones here!

As word got round that the school premises here were available to accommodate groups such as our film-makers on a daily basis, particularly during the summer holiday period, contact was made by the Inverness Art Society. They came out on several occasions over the years and were always gladly welcomed. There was something here, they found, to catch the eye of every kind of artist—croft houses, the Mill, ruins, hills, trees, burns, loch water. They would spread out over a wide area and could work all day undisturbed. Some would come back the following day to finish off drawings or paintings. If the weather broke they could find shelter in the big schoolroom. A picnic lunch could be taken by the fire. Many were intrigued by the feel of the old place, the aura of the drama of school life which had been played out there—the rewards and punishments, the bickerings and laughter, summer sun streaming through the big windows on the south side, winter storms raging outside to the north. Some people would make sketches of the old furniture in the room. One architect member did a most remarkable study of the less conspicuous back part of the building. To my great joy, one summer I found a picture called 'Mrs Stewart's Garden' in the Society's annual exhibition.

Chapter
Nine

Over the next few years we had little time to work on things about the house. We didn't want to make many changes, anyway. We preferred to look and listen, to make the place speak out on its own. It rapidly began to make itself heard. Its Victorian aura was everywhere—in the high-mantled fireplaces in every room, in the low-slung, back-breaking sink with its brass taps in the scullery, in the porch with its double outer door, and inner door with panelled glass. Here and there were signs of former tenants of modern times—the red-painted floor boards in the kitchen, the draught excluders round door-jambs and window-frames. We had long learned to live with draughts. Sometimes we felt an old Victorian draught-screen would have been an asset, when sitting in the Victorian-style room of an evening in winter. In the bedroom we mostly favoured the fresh cool air on the brow, as long as the covers didn't slip off the bed. By day we wore several layers of wool, as we had done in our croft house. This way we managed to avoid most of the colds which seemed to afflict friends from town who came to visit. Their homes, of course, were so well insulated and double-glazed that they expected to live in shirt-sleeves indoors. Somehow or other we kept the frost away, with old-fashioned methods —bales of straw at the water inlet and outlet, small lamps at vulnerable places inside. Old nylons, we found, made good insulation for pipes at risk. When time allowed, we papered one bedroom afresh, and touched up the paintwork in the kitchen and scullery.

As each spring came round it was the garden that absorbed our energies. Every year we came on something new—little clusters of snow-drops emerging from under piles of leaves, woodruff carpeting the ground beneath the huge birches, a rock garden almost completely overgrown with bishop weed and couch grass. Each discovery was hailed with jubilation. We knew the work would be endless, but that didn't matter, for each bit accomplished was a satisfaction in itself. As a plot was cleared in the shelter of the west wall, friends with established gardens would give us great clumps of perennials—lupins, blue geranium, marguerites, lysimachia, scarlet poppies and my all-time favourite—pink astrantia. We constructed a makeshift cold frame out of old windows we found on a scrap-heap and grew wallflower, sweet william, marigolds, all the old-fashioned flowers, from seed. Meantime, tatties, onions, roots and salad crops were flourishing in some well-manured plots of their own.

I had been teaching in Inverness for several years when it was decided that the High School should have an Outdoor Centre. Many schools in the area were establishing such centres. And where better to set one up than in the old school at Abriachan? On first hearing the news we were slightly perturbed. Would the peace and quiet we prized so highly be shattered by the shouting and skirmishing of hordes of the young let loose from the bonds of the classroom? We dwelt on the prospect at length, as we singled the carrots and staked the peas up at the top of the garden. The apples would go, that was one sure thing. The branches of the old tree overhung the playground. Its fruit had always disappeared in days gone by. The children would grab the apples long before they were ripe and discard most of them, half eaten, along the roadside. After a while we began to think, well, it would be good to have the children about the place again. It had been built for such as them. There was plenty of space in the old playground and there were the hills...

That first summer small groups came out in the mini-bus. An art class would spend a day sketching. A gym class would go orienteering. Then the woodwork class got busy making bunk-beds so that people could stay overnight or for a weekend. The accommodation was primitive—cold water in the cloakroom, outside loos, cooking on Calor gas in the 'Home Economics' room. The hill country, with its remaining croft lands, was a revelation to many of the children. Living only ten miles away, in the small town of Inverness, many of them had never ventured further than the local football ground or the canal banks. Some of them were apprehensive at first, as the orphans from Glasgow often were, looking at the vast spaces of hill and sky around them, afraid of getting lost, of a wild fox leaping from the gloom of the trees, even of ants and spiders in the heather. Going to the outside loos after dusk was a dreaded venture. More than once a small boy crashed from his top bunk on to the hard wooden floor. But after several outings fears generally subsided and the days spent in the hills were relished. To come on a young roe-deer, a tiny calf, almost hidden in the bracken or heather and to be told 'Don't touch her. Her mother will be back.

She won't like the smell of human hands on her calf'—this was learning in a real sense, learning at first hand how animals live, how they respond to humans, how to respect them, not look on them as prey. Then there was the day the boys out orienteering almost stumbled on a nest of young hen-harriers and had to dodge the irate mother's beak. And the time they stood to watch black-cock 'on the lek' and the unbelievably fierce battle the birds engaged in when the females arrived. To this day men and women appear in the playground or come to the door, their families in tow, recounting to their children the exploits of their youth.

About the time the Field Centre was set up all secondary schools in the Highlands were notified of a scheme sponsored by the Crofters' Commission, the Civic Trust and the Education Department whereby pupils might 'initiate and carry out projects for the improvement of the appearance of a village' in their area. The scheme was to be completed by 1970, which was to be European Conservation Year. The High School submitted a plan for a project in the area of Abriachan. Villages are not the norm in crofting places. This was evidently understood and the plan was approved. It consisted of four parts—the tidying up of the old burial ground of Kilianan, at the foot of the hill, the cleaning, repairing and painting of the Community Hall, which had been unused for a considerable time, the reconditioning of a former croft house up the road, at Druim, and the establishing of a small croft museum. Trees and flowers were to be planted at the three sites. A small sum of money was to be granted by a Highland landowner to finance the plan.

Two years of steady work lay ahead if all this was to be accomplished in time. A start was made in the autumn—the cutting of weeds, repairing of fences and so on. Then, with the spring, parties of volunteers began coming out at weekends. A woodwork class would stay for a week, or longer, getting practical experience of renewing joists and rafters as they laboured at the croft house. A science class would botanise as they identified flowers and herbs that used to grow there. One day, working at the plot, I heard a voice at my shoulder. I looked up. A big, tough-looking lad was standing there.

'What's that plant you're putting in? I've seen my gran put it in the soup.'

'That's parsley.'

'Parsley? And you get it here?'

'You do.'

He was genuinely interested and amazed and didn't have the growing

47

Planting trees at the Hall

of drugs in mind, only what went into his gran's soup!

Work at the Hall involved parties of girls in doing a thorough cleaning. The dust of years lay everywhere. The windows were encrusted with dirt. In a cupboard ancient encyclopaedias and other books were testimony to the efforts of bygone teachers to provide some sort of 'further education' for interested people. Under the stage was packed away some of the equipment for badminton and other indoor games.

There was an ancient piano, complete with candle-holders, and old paraffin heater and a tea-urn. The Hall had been built by public subscription in the early 1930s. Much hard work was put in on a voluntary basis—the digging of foundations, the erecting of walls and roof—by people in their spare time. It was to be used for social gatherings and also for religious meetings. There was some heated objection to this combined usage by those who thought that no minister should preach in a building which was also used for secular amusement, in particular card-playing. The custom of gambling at cards was still regarded as pernicious, for much ruin had been brought on families over this in the past. However, things settled down eventually, draughts, chess and badminton were played with relish and many concerts and dances enjoyed.

The Second World War brought changes, as it did in most parts. The black-out, the scarcity of heating oil, the absence of many in the Forces, all these things and other factors meant less and less use of the Hall. The Home Guard met there from time to time. There would be an occasional whist drive in an effort to raise funds. The minister would take a Sunday service in summer. But gradually, when most of the trustees died and after the school closed, the Hall became disused. It was good to see it coming back, now, to some sort of life. Woodwork teachers supervised senior boys in the replacing of some roof tiles, the clearing of rhones and down-pipes. Outside painting and the repairing of the door was done when weather permitted. The tumble-down fence round the building was replaced, a job at which the country boys excelled. At one time the surrounds had been used as a 'fank' to house tups awaiting release among the ewes! Gean, rowan, sloe and broom were planted there, in the well-manured ground. A few enthusiasts tried their hand at dry-stane dyking in a effort to repair the wall along the roadside.

It was a happy time. New and different relationships between teachers and pupils, and between the pupils themselves, were established as they worked together, on thought-provoking, yet practical tasks. There was time to talk, to laugh, to be amazed. The realities of country living in older times were a source of endless fascination to the town children. The girls couldn't believe that water had to be fetched from the well before you could fill the kettle, and that a fire had to be lit before it would boil. Also, that your hands came quite clean washed in cold water and a rub with docken leaves took the sting out of a nettle bite! The discoveries were endless.

We came to realise more and more clearly that this was education in a very real sense. Working as a team, each member contributing a portion of the effort, with no time for slacking, seemed to bring out unrealised potential. The 'maths genius' could measure and calculate and work out the number of tiles needed to repair the roof, but equally important was the effort of the 'less able' boy who climbed the ladder and sat fearlessly astride the apex to fix them.

Today we speak of 'work experience' and 'job satisfaction'. In their time here the pupils got a taste of both. To work with no financial incentive, no pay-packet in view, but the sense of achievement as they stood back to look at the mended roof, the fresh-painted walls, the planted garden plot, this seemed to fill a gap in their lives. They seemed to grow with the job, finding a surprising value in themselves, building a fresh identity. For the over-nighters there was a further sense of community, as they gathered round the fire in the old schoolroom after tea, comparing notes on jobs, laughing about mistakes, bantering, attending to cuts and bruises, planning next day's work.

'The stairway up at the croft house...'

'Yon's no' a stairway. Yon's a ladder!'

'That's what you'd think. But it was used. The kids slept up there, in the loft. Bob broke two steps and...'

'No wonder wi' his big feet.'

'Well, we'll need to replace it in the morning. There's work to do up there.'

'Right.'

The croft house had, unbelievably, been used to house hens in deep litter by people running a poultry farm at Leault, the old school croft. We knew this, but until we opened the door and went inside we had little realisation of what it actually entailed. There were two rooms on the ground floor, the 'kitchen' and the 'room', with a small bedroom off the kitchen. Above, there were two rooms with skylights, in the loft. Every inch of floor-space throughout the house was deep in litter—of sawdust, chopped straw, paper and, of course, droppings. This was grand manure for the garden, but the barrowing...! And for years small shovelfuls of litter would fall from behind the upper floor-boards, from under window ledges and other hidden spots.

By the end of the first year's work, with some week-long stays and week-end shifts, things began to take shape. As the momentum increased people were quite happy to come out on a Saturday, when transport could be arranged. The girls would marvel at the amount of sheer hard work their grandmothers must have put in to keep a shine on their pots and to clean their wooden milk churns when water had

Early days working at Druim Croft

to be carried from the well and boiled on the fire. As for trampling blankets in a huge tub, well...they reckoned that might be quite pleasant on a good summer day!

At last, with new joists and floorboards, fireplaces renovated and curtains at the windows, the croft house was ready to be furnished. We had gathered odds and ends from every available source—a table and chairs found abandoned in an old house on ground taken over for forestry, a dresser dumped as being too old-fashioned when shiny plastic came in, a cradle that had been used as a nesting-box when the place had housed hens. Then our own growing collection of plenishings was moved in. It was good to see it in the setting it was made for—the girdle and the kettle by the kitchen fire, the cheese-press and the butter-churn in the cool of the 'room', a Gaelic Bible on the dresser. The peat-spade, the scythe, the pitch-fork and the hay-rake found a place in the steading.

As time went by other items were found, some on dumps, some discarded in overgrown fields. Once we had to check an enthusiastic boy who brought in a scuffler from a nearby croft, an implement which might still have been in use! During the long holidays we would go far afield in the old van collecting what was deemed 'rubbish' by many. A nettle patch by a ruined house was always an area worth searching. If girdles, kettles, iron pots, smoothing irons had been thrown among the nettles, which thrived on them, we reckoned they could be retrieved from their ultimate fate of oblivion, and no harm done. To remove anything found in the vicinity of a living place we always asked permission. Almost invariably it was a case of 'good riddance' or 'glad to get it out of the road'. I remembered from our days on the croft how neighbours were happy to discard work tools when new ones, involving less labour, became available. Heavy iron pots and kettles were replaced by light enamel or aluminium pans. Nothing could really replace the girdle, but plastic eventually did away with cumbersome pails. In the fields new ways of harvesting were introduced. All the labour of the travelling mill and the building of stacks vanished. Only in the smallest places where the huge machinery could not operate did the old methods survive, with the use of scythes to cut the edges, of hay-rakes and pitch-forks as the stacks were built. So it was that many of these old muscle-building tools were discarded and came our way, and we managed to give them some sort of new life as their uses were explained and demonstrated to interested people.

It soon became apparent that in this small house and steading we were going to run out of space to accommodate the growing collection. The Community Hall was now tidied up. In fact, standing there by the roadside, neatly fenced, with the surrounds planted, it looked like the asset it was always meant to be. It was not actually in demand by the community, whose interests lay mainly outwith the area, since communication had become so much easier with access by car to other parts. We approached the one remaining trustee of the hall for permission to house in it the overflow of interesting objects, with historical documents relating to the area, photographs and so on, on the understanding that everything would be removed should people wish the place to revert to its original purpose. This was agreed. A busy programme of preparation then began. Pots were freshly blackleaded, cheese-presses scoured, chairs polished, tools oiled. Photographs were arranged in albums and a label made for every item, with fine lettering produced by the High School's art department. A card index was started to take over the information from the original catalogue. These activities involved many people and increased interest in the project as a whole. The history and geography people began to wonder what they could contribute. A map was made showing walks to places of interest, including sites of prehistoric settlements. The science department sent some seniors out to look at the life of the loch. There were water-birds of many kinds, different species coming and going at different times of year, trout and many smaller fry. Botanists studied the special flora of the area, thrilled to find orchids, sundew and butterwort, lovely flowers growing even in the school playground.

Meantime, work at the old graveyard at Kilianan had been going on quite steadily. Weeds had been dug out and overgrown bushes cut back. We planted a gean, a willow, a laburnum and many daffodils. Snowdrops, primroses and wild hyacinths were there already. There are several inscribed headstones with quite recent dates and many blocks of granite marking the resting-places of the unnamed. One day, a great discovery was made. The clearing-up in a small railed-off enclosure revealed an ancient carved grave-slab. There is a rosette at the head and at the foot a shears. The shears are said to represent the burial-place of a woman. Local tradition has it that this stone marks the grave of a 'Norwegian Princess'. Could she have been a descendant of the Norse people who farmed in nearby Glen Urquhart? According to legend she was beloved by the native families. This would seem to bear out the belief that many Viking invaders eventually settled down peaceably and adopted the Christian faith. The grave is recorded in the annals of the Society of Antiquaries. The moss had covered it.

This burial ground was part of a settlement of the early Celtic church, probably founded by followers of Columba after his journey up the Great Glen, from Iona to Inverness, to confront King Brude in the sixth century. The first attempts at schooling would have been made here. The monks would have taught some likely boys to read and write, to measure and weigh, the first elements of metal and stonework, probably some Latin and a little Greek, so that they could follow acts of worship and praise, as well as the craft of growing plants for food and healing. In later years ambitious boys would attend the school run by the monks at Beauly Priory, some ten miles away. Education, sometimes known as the 'handmaid of religion', was to remain under the aegis of the church for many centuries.

Chapter Ten

When the two years for work on the project were nearly up excitement grew as the 'Day of Judgement' approached. There was a final skirmish of tidying-up, litter was cleared from roadside lay-bys. It was hoped the project really had 'improved the appearance' of the area. Certainly, a derelict croft house, latterly used to accommodate hens, had been restored to something of its former dignity, the Community Hall had been repaired as far as funds would allow, the old graveyard had been cleared and planted, a collection of artefacts and documents relating to the district had been put on display. The adjudicators arrived on a beautiful morning in June. The Crofters Commission, the Scottish Civic Trust and the Education Department were all represented. The headmaster of the High School, several members of staff, the ever-helpful janitor and many of the pupils were there, too, to act as guides at the various sites.

It was a day to lift the heart—a turquoise sky, the birches in fresh leaf, larks rising and falling in ecstatic song. Our visitors must have been glad to leave their desks and paper-work behind and to feel the reality of this hill-land. So many had come to love it as they worked and walked about and looked at things with new sight. Something of its spirit had rubbed off on them, I think. It showed in the quiet, bright smiles, in the quick response to questioning, the touch of pride when comments of praise were made.

When everything had been inspected our visitors were entertained to tea and scones in the outside classroom, now known as the canteen. There was good talk and much laughter as we told the story of our two years' work—how some of the boys had made firm resolves to become joiners or stone-masons or even gardeners, girls had ideas about museum work or even of marrying a crofter! Few had found it hard or boring. There were no speeches made and the project was duly awarded an inscribed plaque.

After the goodbyes, when our visitors had set off for Inverness,

In the croft house at Druim

Edinburgh or beyond and their congratulations were ringing in our ears, we three—the heads of geography and building and myself—who had been largely responsible for organising the project, sat down to consider the situation. We knew this was not the end, but only the beginning of the planned operation. We had created something which would have to be maintained, developed, allowed to grow.

Meantime, our thoughts went, as they often did, to the people whose families had lived and worked here for generations and of whom so few remained *in situ*. Many were scattered in far-off places, but some were probably within reach. Would it be possible, we wondered, to have a reunion? We put a notice in the Inverness paper. Transport could be arranged for a ceilidh in the old school on an evening in September. Come early and stay late, we said. The news spread like wildfire, a happy version of the Fiery Cross! So, on a glorious autumn afternoon, they came, from Perthshire, from England, from Dundee, from the West, as well as from Inverness. We met at the school, then, before the afternoon faded, we made our way up to the croft house at Druim. Not for years had we seen so many walking the road and talking and talking! Some smiles were a little sad, most were wide and happy as the women gathered round the open fire, picking up the huge black kettle, the girdle, the old iron pot and reminiscing about the food they

55

got in their youth. The men were examining the implements in the steading—the ploughs and harrows, scythes and pitch-forks and peat-spades—and remembering the hard labour that had given them mighty appetites and muscles of iron.

The collection in the Hall intrigued them all, too, There, they could see photographs of themselves in school groups. There was much eager identifying of friends and erstwhile enemies. The teachers came in for some caustic comments, though many were remembered happily and there was laughter all round as anecdotes were recounted and happenings recalled. Memories were astonishingly clear. Schooldays must have been tolerable when the thought of them had not been banished from these minds. Then it was into the old schoolroom and more memories evoked. One woman drew a deep breath as she came through the door.

'Ah...' she said, with a smile in her half-closed eyes, 'that's it! It's that smell I remember—the old damp woodwork and the smoke from the fire. That's school on a winter day. We were glad to get in, out of the cold, though the teacher might be glaring at our muddy boots. We didn't care. We'd take what came. We were part of the crowd. It was great!'

So many had come to the reunion that there was no room for a sit-down supper at tables. People were too busy talking, anyway, and happy to be moving about. Soup was taken on the hoof, with sandwiches, sausage-rolls and cakes, baked in the High School kitchen. This was a ceilidh in the real sense of the word, a meeting of folk to exchange news and views and then, when the spirit took them, to sing a song from the heart, to play a tune for the tapping of feet and the forgetting of all worry and care. We made up the fire, somehow we got everyone seated, on chairs, benches or footstools, and a hush came as a woman's voice rose softly. The Gaelic words were strange to some, but many remembered and the chorus was joined with growing confidence and pleasure. Then it was song after song, a spontaneous succession of songs, some sad, some funny, in Gaelic and English and even in Scots. We had a piper, too, and a fiddler and a man to tell tall tales. At last, as some had long journeys to go, there had to be farewells. But first, somehow, a space was cleared and an eightsome danced with all the verve of long-ago schooldays. We joined hands to sing 'Auld Lang Syne'. We couldn't believe this was an ending. Already, on the doorstep, there was talk of the next time.

Chapter
Eleven

In 1971, a year after the completion of the Highland Village Project, the scheme went into a second phase, 'Highland Village 1973', initiated by the Crofters Commission, to be financed by the Highlands and Islands Development Board and the Countryside Commission. This led to the development of parts of the original project—electrical installations for lighting at the croft house and the further planting of the garden there and the publication of a small booklet on the area, with illustrations by pupils of Inverness High School Art Department. The preparation of the booklet involved a fair amount of research into the history of the district. We were lucky enough to have friends whose families came from Abriachan and were only too willing to give us any information they had. The few remaining native inhabitants had for long been telling us of happenings and beliefs, signs and wonders that made the place come as intensely alive for us as it had for them. The transactions of the Gaelic Society of Inverness and of the Inverness Field Club supplied us with the facts of history and of science.

Originally, to primitive people, a site in bare uplands, about 800 feet above sea level, would have been an attractive place to settle. No dense forests meant no hiding place for fierce beasts. Birch, alder, gean, rowan and scrub grew in sheltered hollows to provide timber and firing. Game, berries and nuts were in abundance. In the nearby loch were fish and waterfowl for the taking. Life could have been quite pleasant. Enemies would have been spotted from afar and warned off promptly.

As time went by these early settlers gradually ceased to depend entirely on hunting and gathering for sustenance and began to cultivate small patches of cleared ground. Signs of this activity can be seen in several places today. Probably a primitive form of barley would have been grown, to provide meal. In the early part of the Christian era news of the teaching of the monks at Kilianan would doubtless have reached the uplands. The arts of husbandry would be learnt and practised, with much benefit to the community.

The first mention of Abriachan in written history occurs about the beginning of the thirteenth century, when it is described as being in the possession of the Byssets of Lovat. These Byssets, great benefactors of the church, founded Beauly Priory. The power of the church grew steadily and among the lands gifted to it at about this time was the Barony of Kinmylies—'including Easter and Wester Abriachan'. In 1334 John, Bishop of Moray, gave to Sir Robert Lauder, Governor of Urquhart Castle—'for his manifold services to our said church'—'a half davoch of land at Abriachy' upon payment of an annual feu of '4 merks sterling'. Sir Robert's successors resigned the lands and they were then granted to Alexander, brother of King Robert III, known as the 'Wolf of Badenoch', on 3rd February 1386. We have often wondered if the 'Wolf' roamed about the hills here and whether he pillaged the remains of the little settlement at Kilianan. By 1451 the lands had been returned to the church. Then, in 1544, Bishop Hepburn granted a charter to Hugh Fraser, Lord Lovat. A hundred years later they were sold to Colonel Hugh Fraser of Kinnaries, whose son resold them to Ludovic Grant. In 1704 they were put under wadset (mortgage) for 10,000 merks to James and Alexander of Reelig, who conveyed the wadset in 1730 to Evan Baillie of Dochfour, a great friend of Lovat of the '45. This wadset was redeemed by Sir J. Grant, and Abriachan became part of the Seafield Estates. In 1946 it was split up and sold to tenants and others.

This is the story of buying and selling recorded in the musty old charters. The lives of the people went on year in, year out, no matter to whom they owed allegiance or paid rent. They had to fight for survival against the forces of nature, against invaders in the Wars of Independence, in their allegiance to their chiefs in inter-clan battles, in the harrying after Culloden. The two great civilising factors in their lives were their attachment to the church, from its beginnings at Kilianan, and, later, their belief in the value of education.

Records show that, in 1589, Maclellans and Mackillroys were the dominant people. These names, however, died out later when Frasers, Macdonalds, Grants, Chisholms, Mackenzies and Macleans became the most numerous families. Some of the Macdonalds are said to be descendants of those who sought refuge in the fastnesses of Abriachan after the massacre of Glencoe. Abiding by the old Highland custom of hospitality, the people seldom denied welcome to the landless and the outcast which the old feuding clan system threw up. Abriachan had always been looked upon as a sanctuary. After the massacre of Culloden it is likely that Government troops carried out atrocities in the area, as they did much harrying in the Great Glen. Tradition has it that one part—Corryfoyness, where there was a settlement of five families— escaped the pillage. It was, and still is, comparatively inaccessible. The going would have tried those men in their cumbersome uniforms, carrying their cumbersome guns.

Today, even Frasers and Macdonalds are few and far between. But the sanctuary element remains, as incomers from many parts seek to establish roots in the quiet of hill and moor and native wood.

Abriachan had always been a self-contained community. Its geographical position, above the fault known as the Great Glen, on a green shelf smoothed out as the ice slid down, gives it a certain inaccessibility. The people had, perforce, to become skilled in the arts and crafts of daily living. The skills of the chase came instinctively and there was plenty of prey. Materials for the building of small houses were to hand— granite and whinstone for walls, timber and heather thatch for roofing. In later years many young men developed their skills in building while waiting to inherit the family croft. In this way the community was blessed with many full-fledged craftsmen—joiners and especially masons, as the abundance of superb stone inspired their work. There were shoe-makers, too, working in hide, and tailors. Tailoring would have developed, naturally enough, from the craft of weaving. Women, also, were skilled weavers and spinners. Blacksmiths plied their trade. Young women often went to the harvesting on big farms in the south and men to the shepherding, to earn something of a wage. And, of course, there was always sale for a drop or two from the hidden 'still'.

Wedding gatherings were held in the garnished barn, with a white flag flying from the house chimney. Funerals, too, were conducted in the house of the bereaved family and were occasions of companionship in sorrow, the coffin carried on friendly shoulders to the burial ground. The young found ways of enjoying time out of school after work. In summer there was dancing at the crossroads by the bridge, with music on the mouth-organ or the 'box', and fishing in the small lochs hidden high in the hills, and swimming. Winter was for shinty to get the circulation going and ceilidhs in the long evenings. There was plenty to do within the bounds of home.

There was no church after the decay of the early chapel at Kilianan, but there was always a prayer meeting on Sundays, either in the school or out-of-doors. At one time, in the 1920s, Evangelists would put up a marquee on a piece of spare ground, hold services and visit houses.

The corn-mill was often a centre of activity, with comings of loads of oats and goings of freshly-ground meal. Sometimes volunteers were needed to turn the water on or off at the sluice up at the loch.

Until comparatively recently the community had all the familiars of so many places in the Highlands, first and foremost a bard. He was Thomas Macdonald (1822-86), son of John Macdonald and Helen Maclachlan, daughter of an early schoolmaster. He composed many poems and songs, some in a sarcastic vein, which he may have learnt from his father-in-law, who often used satire as a way of upbraiding people for wrongdoings. He also wrote, in the old bardic way, praise poems for people deemed worthy of praise—one for Major Grant of the local laird's family and one for Baillie W. G. Stuart. A song in praise of Glen Urquhart has also survived, but poems of his are difficult to find, as, on his death-bed, he is said to have asked for them to be destroyed. Religious teaching at the time perhaps considered the writing of verse an ungodly pursuit and he wanted to be right with his Maker. I think the compositions probably came to him as naturally as music and song always came to the Gaels.

Also in the community were several women who had the 'second sight'. One, in particular, often wished this faculty had escaped her, for her 'sightings' were always of sad things, forebodings of illness or death, which weighed heavily on her spirit. Another woman, remembered still by one or two of the oldest people, was reputed to be a witch. I think she was really a slightly eccentric old lady, who lived alone in a one-room house, the walls of which still stand, built for her as a 'granny-house'. When the thatch gave way one night of storm she stayed quite happily in the shelter of a huge black umbrella till a repairer arrived. If she was a witch I think she must have been a white witch, for she was always good to children, giving them a scone if they passed nearby, nursing them through whooping-cough or measles.

As the last of the old folk go, so the belief in magic will go with them—the faculty of seeing the 'wee folk' in a grassy hollow under the crags, those fairy folk who took the milk you put out for them so that they wouldn't harm your cattle. There will be no more fear of the 'evil eye' that could put a curse on man or beast, or of the kelpie that might lure you to ride on its back into black depths of the loch. Equally, there will be no more faith in the beneficence of the rowan tree that guards your door. And who will walk widdershins three times around the house, then bow to the new moon in her slim splendour?

These things added poetry to the prose of everyday life. The children of today have other sources of magic, I know. I just wish they would come dancing off the screen and be there—on the grass, among the trees, by the loch shore, in the wind and snow. Outer space is where the dreams are now. But inner space needs the young, with their energy and drive, to salvage it from exploitation and distress.

Back in the seventies, when Environmental Studies became popular, students began coming out to look at what the area had to offer. Geologically and botanically it was interesting, they reckoned. It is known as a 'hanging valley', left behind as the ice-floes sank into the Great Glen. Rose-red granite, smoothed to the shine of marble, had long been quarried on the slope. It was used for gravestones as well as for building. There is blue clay, and here and there the glitter of pegmatite. One specific mineral—blue 'Abriachanite'—is found in places among the granite. As there has been a minimal use of artificial fertilisers over the years, there is quite a profusion of wild plants, in particular those which thrive in the damp acidity. Gean and bird cherry blossom in spring. In autumn there is the splendour of birch leaves, bracken and heather. A photographic record of the flora was made at this time, using a telescopic lens. It is hoped the flowers will continue to bloom, in spite of acid rain, nuclear fall-out and all the perils of today. In some years fungi are plentiful—boletus along the roadside, chanterelle in favoured spots among the birches. Wildlife is comparatively undisturbed. Fox, badger, pine marten, roe and red deer and a few red squirrel live in reasonable peace, along with buzzard, grouse, kestrel, heron, waterfowl and many summer birds. Peewits, the long looked-for heralds of spring, are scarce now and there is a sad lack of larks, as traditional methods of cultivation have all but disappeared.

For the students there was always the question of land use. Large tracts were being planted with conifers. Was this a good thing or a bad thing, they queried, as they trudged around with binoculars, cameras and notebooks. Still today, this is a question which hangs in the air. But at least native trees are holding their own. Birch still stand among the pines, rowan and gean thrust their colours through the everlasting green. Hazel and alder appear unbidden wherever their seed falls easy. The plantings had to be fenced, of course, to keep out marauding animals, and deer-fenced at that, which meant that access for orienteering, or even for walkers, bird-watchers or botanists, was limited. Camping was not allowed as there was the fear of fire. Today, now that the trees are established, limited access is possible, there are stiles here and there, but still the lack of freedom to roam is felt. The old people remember when the hills were the common grazing ground for sheep, cattle in summer and horses—not the fine riding horses that graze the fields now, but the sturdy garrons that did the work of the crofts all week and had their Sundays to rest in the sweet hill grass.

Eventually, of course, trees have to be felled or sold, or both. It is hoped, however, that one small area which was designated an 'amenity planting' and is very attractive, can be saved and become an asset for the community.

Meanwhile the school was still in use as a Field Centre for the High School. Over the next years it was made available to parties of Scouts, Boys Brigaders and others for weekend or week-long use. Some of these parties came from more distant towns and did not know the area at all. Some came armed with air guns and fearsome-looking knives, obviously hoping to go hunting. Shots sometimes whistled perilously near anyone working in the garden! We had some moments of trepidation, too, when the more adventurous wandered off into the mud flats on the far side of the loch. And we had to keep a close watch when sparks were streaking from the old schoolhouse chimney as they dried their clothes in the course of the night. But we, and the old school, survived! It was nice, too, to be surprised by the appearance of flowers or a wee bottle of Scotch on the doorstep on the morning of an early departure!

As work on the project became gradually less demanding we were able to indulge our wish for some of the old self-sufficiency we had had on the croft. We acquired Bridget, a loveable white nanny-goat with amber eyes, who gave us ample milk on a diet of docken, willow-herb, nettles and grass, with a supplement of mash in the morning; half-a-dozen chickens, and five hives of bees. The chickens settled in quickly and soon produced a surplus of eggs. The bees, also, made more honey then we or our friends could eat and we were able to sell some to eager customers in the town. In older times the schoolmaster always had what amounted almost to a croft—a garden, the 'keep' of a cow and a share in the hill grazing. So we were carrying on the tradition!

Over the next few years the character of Abriachan began to change. Whereas when we arrived, some 25 years previously, it had been considered a somewhat wild and remote place, it was now, with the car, or two-car family, being reckoned a very desirable place to live. Commuting to work in Inverness was quite possible, since the road had been up-graded, with adequate passing-places. There were even litter-bins at likely picnic spots. Houses were being renovated and new ones built.

At the same time the school was in less demand as a Field Centre, as other, better-equipped places were opening up in different parts. Outside 'loos' and cold water washing facilities were considered too primitive for modern, town-bred youth. In summer an art class would come out for a day's sketching, gymnasts would do some 'jogging'. A party of boys with a 'technical' teacher would carry out a repair job at the croft house or paint the roof of the playground shelter.

As staff changes in the High School occurred, interest in the maintenance of the project naturally dwindled. The newcomers to the place had, of course, little knowledge of what had been going on. Slowly, as more people arrived in Abriachan, a demand grew for some sort of meeting-place for the occasional gathering. The school was there, it had electric lighting and at least an open fire for warmth, so gradually it reverted to one of its original roles, that of a place for religious assembly. The schoolmasters of old had always been expected to act as catechist for the whole community, to take a Sunday school for adults as well as for children and sometimes to preach a sermon. In older times the 'big' room was filled with desks, into which men and women of all shapes and sizes would cram themselves when they came on a Sabbath evening to hear the sermon. Very attentive they would be and often very critical of the prowess of the preacher. There would be serious discussion of the contents of his discourse in many homes later on. A minister from one of the nearby parishes would come at regular intervals to take the service. This custom was now revived, with the congregation accommodated more comfortably than hitherto, on chairs, and warmed by portable gas heaters as well as the fire. It was good to hear the old hallowed words sounding round the room again and the voices rising and falling in the long-familiar psalms and hymns. These had always been church lands, as we have seen. The old Sanctuary stone still stands. Now one could feel the serenity of the past echoing clearly into the future. A cup of tea, a practical offering of which the monks of old would surely have approved, was served before the minister took his sometimes, in winter, precarious journey home. Then, all the little bickerings and arguments, inevitable in any small community, set aside, people would gather round the fire to exchange news and arrange lifts back to the more outlying places.

The next custom to be revived was that of holding a party for the children at Christmas. I remembered those held when the school was still open and the thrill of coming out of an evening of fierce frost into the light and warmth of a blazing fire, the huge, dark green tree in the corner, with its shiny tinsel making it magic and the aroma of steaming tea and hot pastry. There would be a gigantic hammering on the door and an enormous 'Santa' would appear, his sack brimming with small, gleefully awaited presents. There were round games like 'I sent a letter to my love and on the way I dropped it'—this always engendered a tingle of excitement—other singing games, musical chairs and 'pass the parcel', all played equally enthusiastically by children and adults.

As plans were made for the renewal of festivities we had to cater for the children of today. Christmas never fails. The tree was there and the fire and the party food. Some of the old games were played as happily as ever, and there was music for eightsomes and Strip-the-Willow. The Dashing White Sergeant pranced around. Mothers slow-waltzed with toddlers or babes-in-arms. Granddads sat it out, reminiscing quietly. We had songs from our one native Gaelic singer and music from a brother and sister on the pipes.

As the Christmas party became an established tradition again many talents were uncovered. Plays were written and performed with great acclaim. More instruments were played—the guitar, the whistle, the clarsach. So music was there again, as it had been some fifty years before, when the Abriachan School Choir was famous for winning prizes at the Mod and in all the local competitions. Until recently the old people remembered the occasion when the bus driver, joining in the excitement of a big win at Oban, missed the turning at Spean Bridge on the way home and had to make the journey the long way round, while anxious parents waited all night at the foot of the hill with pony and trap to take the tired children home!

New Year was, and still is, celebrated in houses. One house in particular, that of our oldest native of Abriachan, had become the 'ceilidh' house at this time, crammed to the door, with twenty or thirty people queuing for the warm room and a seat at the fire. He entertains us with the Gaelic songs of his youth. We join the choruses and the young musicians of today keep the music going on instrument after instrument. Drams circulate and companionship is enjoyed. Later, tea is brewed and by then the New Year is well on its way in. Not long since the oldest people here would recall the days the 'old' New Year was celebrated, before the calendar was changed. This meant that festivities could go on till, and after, January 12th!

Chapter
Twelve

As I lived practically next door to the two main parts of the project—the collection in the Hall and the croft house up the road—I was naturally made key-holder and custodian of these places, a charge which I accepted gladly enough. It entailed, of course, opening up and explaining things to interested visitors, as we had already been doing, on a much smaller scale, with our collection in the out-building. My husband helped out with this on many occasions, when I had to be elsewhere. Sadly, some of the older girls who had been really interested in the collection, who had industriously cleaned black pots and been willing to come out on a Saturday to act as guides, were due to leave school. Some came during the holidays, when transport could be arranged. We encouraged a few from more junior classes to learn the job, but not many were as interested as those who had worked throughout the two years. There was a revival of interest in the Art Department which produced some beautifully lettered information sheets, as well as labels for the increasing number of objects. A couple of talented teachers in the Department spent part of their summer holiday in a caravan arranging things in attractive settings. We had been noting down the provenance of the various items as they were acquired and now began drawing up a rather more ambitious catalogue. It fell short of being really professional but served its purpose adequately for a number of years.

We clearly had none of the expertise of museum curators. In fact, I avoided as far as possible using the term 'museum', as it still resonated, for me, with the sounds of being marshalled with a group of young contemporaries into enormous buildings full of enormous stuffed animals and innumerable objects in glass cases, when I would much rather have been out on a hill-walk or a day at the sea! I still prefer to use the word 'collection', and all the things in the collection, or nearly all, can be handled, examined and some can be made to work. Of course, care has to be taken that heavy or sharp objects are treated with discretion.

Judging from the comments in the Visitors' Books over the years most people appreciate this way of presentation. We have had visitors from all parts of the world and have enjoyed their entries in the column headed 'Remarks'. One Indian lady said of the implements and tools they were 'just like India today'. A lady from Mexico was thrilled to see the old cooking-pots. 'My mother has one of those' she exclaimed delightedly. Could a Highland emigrant family have settled in her village, or did the foundry export its pots, we wondered? The French most often recorded their appreciation in their own language— 'Petit musée plein de choses interéssantes'. 'Ce musée m'a aidé à comprendre l'Écosse'. These entries and the many conversations we had with visitors were a great encouragement and made us feel the work was really worthwhile. Even small contacts made with other parts seem to diminish the gulf that can divide.

The happiness of the reunion of former residents of Abriachan inspired us to have a gathering of local people at Hallowe'en. We remembered so clearly the Hallowe'en of our first year on the croft. Then , when treats were fewer and further between, the children would prepare well ahead for a real night out, incognito, when they could get away with all sorts of tricks and harmless enough mischief. Two or three came to our door wearing unimaginably weird disguises. Only a laugh or a giggle could disclose a slight clue to identity. We left them to the anonymity they wanted, admired their amazing turnip lanterns, heard a verse of song and thrust sweets and apples into eager, grimy hands. They played no tricks on us but we heard tales of bygone days when a divot would be thrown down a lum to made the fire smoke, the pony would be loused from the stable and sent careering down the brae, tatties would be thrown at the roof to make the slates clatter. It could all be blamed on the evil spirits abroad that night!

The party we planned was to be a tame affair compared to the doings of earlier days, but the children brought turnip lanterns and the best one won a prize. They dooked for apples and snatched at hanging treacle scones. There was tea and cakes and a ceilidh. Three Abriachan brothers entertained us with their wonderful fiddle playing. A piper gave us a pibroch that took our thoughts to Skye, and beyond. The schoolroom, with its high ceiling, was acoustically good. We asked for more music, and more...Then we had songs and stories that made us laugh. So the evil spirits were kept at bay and in the morning we welcomed the saintly ones.

Chapter
Thirteen

The year 1972 marked the centenary of the famous Act which brought education under the aegis of the State and out of the direct control of the church. Religion still had a part to play with morning prayers and hymns, Bible classes and School Chaplains. Today, of course, there is less observance of these remaining traditions. School Boards were set up, comprising elected members, mostly professional people, with powers to promote the building of large new schools and to enforce strict attendance by the pupils. Board members could, and often did, visit the schools, although they were not regarded as official Inspectors. Sometimes they fell out with teachers.

Schooling, in the terms of this Act, was made compulsory between the ages of 5 and 13. Twenty years later fees were abolished. In the towns, large numbers of children, whose families had migrated from the country, were taken off the streets. For those still living in the country there was now a chance to take advantage of a sound primary education, in adequate surroundings, with adequate facilities, and the possibility of obtaining a scholarship for further study and entry to the professions. Among the new, fine schools built at this time was the one in Abriachan.

In the towns, many Victorian school buildings are disappearing. Glasgow, in particular, has a wealth of magnificent schools. It is to be hoped that some, at least, can be saved to serve acceptable purposes. One which I visited in the old town ten years ago had a special interest as the Alma Mater of several members of the family. It was in use as a Community Centre. When I next went to see and photograph it, as a keepsake, it had gone, along with a neighbouring sandstone tenement. One outer wall remained, where the words 'Girls', 'Boys', and 'Infants' could still be read, carved into the stone. Probably on my next visit I shall find a huge uninspiring office block rearing up on the site.

School buildings similar to the one in Abriachan are to be found all over the Highlands. Mostly they stand serene, though deprived of the life they were intended for. Many have been converted to a variety of purposes—as dwelling-houses, as social centres, as craft shops. The one we first knew, those years ago, where Helen was a pupil and the learning and the playing went on quietly, noisily, happily, is now a residence of note. Through the high windows of the 'big' room one can catch a glimpse of pictures on the walls, of tall indoor plants, of ornaments on the ledges, things of beauty, all of them, but where is that feel of contained vibrancy, of young energy waiting to burst forth into life? It has taken itself off, of course, to other parts, with the children. The playground is there, the shelter, even the old toilets, but there is an emptiness all around. The children who would have gone to these schools find themselves bussed to bigger places, cut off from their roots, ill-adapted to the different life-style of their new companions.

Recalling the importance of the great Education Act of 1872, we decided to celebrate its centenary by mounting a display in the museum showing the history of the school here. We already had a list of head teachers and some accounts of visits by Inspectors in times prior to 1872. We had been given copies of photographs of school groups and we had access to the school Log Books, kept in the archives of the Highland Council in Inverness. I remembered consulting these when doing a paper during my training in Aberdeen. We now had recourse to them again and found them a fascinating source of information.

The keeping of a weekly record of progress and attendance in school was made compulsory by the new Act. It was stipulated that the book should be 'stoutly bound', consisting of not less than 500 pages and that no entries of a personal or critical nature should be made.

From the entries, particularly the early ones, a picture emerges, not only of what went on in school, but of the life and times of the community as a whole. There is mention of storms, of illness, of deaths and funerals, of outings to celebrate events in the wider world, of the visits of Attendance Officers, of the arrival of orphan children, of the problems of bilingualism and of the need for children to help with work about the crofts. The entries also reflect the nature of the headmaster making them. Some later ones are frankly tedious to read, repetitious and dull. Many show a lively interest and compassion for the families as well as the children. Some contain hints of rebellion against authorities reluctant to meet demands such as an improved water supply, drainage of the playground and so on.

The first entry in the Abriachan School Log Book, made by headmaster Alexander Maclean in February 1875, when there were 70 children on the roll, states that attendance was irregular owing to storms

Inspector's report on Abriachan School in 1876

and sickness and that by the end of April of that year children were being kept at home to help with potato-planting. The summer vacation, or 'harvest play', was from 20th August to 2nd October, which would cover the hay and corn harvests. They were still lifting potatoes till the middle of November. These absences were understandable in a crofting area, where the gathering-in of supplies was of prime importance, but the situation must have been frustrating for a young, keen schoolmaster like Maclean.

On December 25th, attendance was good and on January 1st it was 'very good'. On January 8th there were 'New Year holidays'. They must have been keeping the 'old' new year and probably ignoring Christmas.

The first Inspector's report under the new regime, issued on 25th July 1876, states that '[this school] is taught with great ability and very good results, most creditable in the circumstances'. It goes on: 'all should have slates and a quantity should belong to the school for occasional use and slate racks and pen-holders in desks should be provided'. His report on the subjects taught went thus: 'Dictation—good. Arithmetic —good. Notation—good. Industrial work—good'. Then he notes 'arrangements should be made for having music taught'.

School Inspectors had been going their rounds since 1840. Initially they were supposed to visit five schools a week. This was quite clearly impossible in the Highlands, where they sometimes had to travel on horseback, were often held up by bad weather at ferries, and so on. Many good stories have been told of their adventures. Though the going was hard they were most often accommodated in comfort in manse or inn, when they could not reach the schoolhouse. They found headmasters of many diverse kinds and were presented with many and diverse problems, but it was an interesting life for men of the right calibre.

Most often their visits were anticipated. Some headmasters would post a boy as look-out to warn of their imminent arrival. Occasionally they would make a surprise visit so as to obviate over-preparation, when pupils would learn passages by heart and be unable to answer questions on the content!

In 1864 a 'Revised Code' for education had been issued, in which 'payment by result' made grants available for proficiency in various subjects. The standards required were prescribed by the authorities, in what amounted almost to a national curriculum. For instance, in the Three Rs:

Junior pupils
Reading: Monosyllables
Writing: Capital and small letters
Arithmetic: Figures to 20, oral addition and subtraction to 10

Senior pupils
Reading: A news paragraph
Writing: A news paragraph
Arithmetic: Practice and bills

In 1950 the system of 'payment by result' was discontinued. Inspectors today work in an advisory capacity, with less fault-finding. In Mr Maclean's day their visits were in the nature of an ordeal for teachers and pupils. Most often a day, or several days, of holiday came after the inspection.

In his report of August 1877 the Inspector states 'This school continues to be taught with the same vigour and sweep'. This phrase brings a picture of the master and of the Inspector, I think! He describes the children as 'tidy, earnest and thorough and very willing'. The discipline, he says, is 'good, but might be more genial' and says ' the books are still too advanced'. He is evidently pleased so see that 'music was begun this year.' He is worried about attendance and says 'this should receive the Board's attention' and goes on: 'the need of a monitor should be considered by the Board'.

Schools were often closed from a Thursday to the following Monday for 'Communion week'. This was an important time in the Free Church calendar when people came from far and wide to attend services, often held in the open air in summer, when congregations could meet at a sheltered spot on a hillside. This happened in August of the year 1878, and again in November. On October 12th, Mr McGillivray, Mr Maclean's predecessor, who still lived in the former schoolhouse, had called in to the school and had 'urged upon the children the necessity of attending school as the Board was determined to prosecute all defaulters'.

During the following winter severe weather kept attendance down, but in his summer report the Inspector says 'Very good results notwithstanding the severe winter. Arithmetic: Very good indeed. Fingers should not be used'. Perhaps fingers were a better form of calculator! Mental arithmetic certainly kept young wits active in those days!

Mr Maclean clearly had problems to overcome in the running of his school, but he must have had pupils in whose progress he could rejoice. In a notebook kept by John Fraser, of Abriachan, in 1878, we find, beautifully written, a Latin vocabulary, parsing of the sentence, 'How do you do?' and an essay on the 'Life of Cromwell', marked '9 v.g.' and a letter to an imaginary recipient which reads: 'Abriachan has greatly improved since the last ten years' and goes on to mention a new road, the new school, a new mill and the planting of a wood. Less tidily written, perhaps added much later, after he left school, are the words of songs such as 'Wae's me for Prince Charlie', 'The Last Rose of Summer'. 'A Man's a Man for a' that'. There are also some in Gaelic. At the end, in pencil, are a few shorthand symbols. Along with the

Abriachan since ten years.

Abriachan 20th Feb. 1882.

Dear Sir,

there is no doubt that Abriachan + has greatly improved since the last ten years. Perhaps the most important of these improvements is the new road which was constructed several years ago. This road is a great benediction to the place; and serves for the purpose of carrying on traffic. A few years ago a new school-house was erected, where daily instructions are given. We have a new mill also built, which saves considerable trouble from going elsewhere to grind our meal. There was a wood planted three or four years ago, above Balmore, and we hope when old enough it will supply us partically with fire, &c, as well as protect us from the severe northern winds laden with keen frost from the Polar regions.

I am, Dear Sir, yours truly
John Fraser.

11

Extract from an Abriachan student's notebook

notebook is a tattered copy of Thomson's *Seasons*. One wonders what he made of that...

Mr Maclean stayed only five years in the school. His successor was Mr Evan Munro who arrived on 27th October 1880, when very few children were in attendance. Probably they were at the potato harvest. The following January and February saw extremely severe weather but on the 19th February we read that 'the Latin class is making considerable progress' and on the 26th there is recorded a 'great improvement in the reading of Gaelic'. So things were moving along, and from these entries we see that there is some flexibility in the teaching of Gaelic and of Latin. In April children were kept at home 'in planting a wood at Caiplich'. This would have been work for the laird and presumably there would have been some payment made to the parents.

The summer report says 'the school has made a very good start under the new teacher...very creditable after the severe winter. Music somewhat rough. The grant for geography and history is allowed with some hesitation'. In the period 1881-82 snow-storms are reported in October and in April. Attendance was badly affected. Some of the children had to walk considerably more than two miles and waterproof clothing was really non-existent. In April 1883 we have the first report of infectious illness—measles—afflicting the children. It amounted to an epidemic and in May the school was closed for disinfection. Brought up in the pure hill air the children did not build up immunity to infectious illnesses and many such diseases became killers. Young men joining the army often succumbed to measles and its complications in camps in the south.

On June 16th 1883 we read 'Lessons not so well prepared as most of the children required to herd before and after school'. With crops growing apace in the unfenced fields it was, of course, essential to keep the cows and sheep at bay. The children must have spent many happy hours tending the beasts and cheerfully forgetting most of their book-learning! Then, on November 3rd the entry reads 'There being only ten present school was dismissed at 1pm. The Default Officer went through the district on Thursday and Friday. The people, however, will not send their children to school until the potatoes are lifted'.

A report dated January 12th 1884 states: 'with 95 pupils on the roll this school has an average attendance of 40. These figures require no comment. The work is remarkably well done... and the discipline is all that could be required'. With a smaller number of children the teacher no doubt found it easier to maintain higher standards of work and discipline. But the absentees must have suffered.

In April of the year 1884 the Earl of Seafield died. His forebears had encouraged education, providing help in the building of the old school and schoolhouse. The school was closed on the day of his funeral.

That autumn Mr Munro, perhaps discouraged by the poor attendance at school, took his teaching elsewhere and on the 6th November Mr Donald Mackay arrived. He was a man who really understood the people better than his predecessors and he was to stay at the school for 22 years. He is still remembered with affection by descendants of the pupils he cared for. On December 26th he notes 'the children coming from Caiplich are very backward—the want of English and irregular attendance account for this'. Next year, on February 3rd, Donald Fraser, from Caiplich, was appointed Monitor during the winter months. Soon afterwards he got a job in Caithness as clerk in the Highland Railway, the great new enterprise that was opening up the country. On April 10th, Catherine Macdonald from Bracklish was admitted. She 'comes a distance of between 3 and 4 miles'. Ten days later he notes: 'Admitted Cath Ann and Emily Fraser, 7 years of age, from Inverness Poor House and lodged with a family in Caiplich'. This is the first mention of 'boarded-out' children. On June 12th we read 'Admitted Cath and Mary Ann Fraser from Corifoines. These girls have been taught to read by their father and they can speak English which is a very great advantage'. On December 11th the entry reads 'Attendance very good. Almost all the children have come back to school now, but those who have been away since the end of spring forgot a great deal of what they acquired previously'. It is clear that the rule of compulsion to make the children attend school could not really be made to apply in the Highlands, in spite of the work of the Defaulting Officers.

1886 was an exceedingly cold winter. On March 19th the record states: 'Most elderly persons do not recollect such a continuation of stormy weather'. On April 16th this, by way of compensation: 'This evening the children and also many of their parents and friends had a social entertainment of tea etc. in the school room. There were about 200 present. Mr McIver, Inverness, showed a great variety of views by the Magic Lantern, which interested the children immensely. A most enjoyable evening was spent. We had no school today'.

On May 21st this extract shows another side of the attendance problem: 'Attendance fair...above Standard III irregular, just day about, when one is at school another must stay at home, but that is a much better plan than to keep one child away altogether'.

So the year went on until in December: 'the drift was so blinding on Thursday that the children from Caiplich and others far away did not venture to come and it may be noted that these children are exceedingly hardy and brave to face a stormy day'. These were the conditions prevailing in the winter of 1955 when Helen could not reach school from Caiplich for several weeks.

This year 1886 is memorable, of course, as the year of the passing of the Act assuring security of tenure for crofters on their holdings. After months of deliberation and the recording of reams of evidence it was deemed that justice must prevail in this regard. It certainly gave the people much encouragement to improve the land they held, with the knowledge that they could pass it on unhindered to their descendants. They still did not have enough land and there were still restrictions. Poaching a rabbit for the pot was still a punishable offence. But hope was in the air.

The following February, in 1887, a six-year-old boy died of diphtheria. In March there was 'hooping cough' and 'what is called German measles'. The parents dreaded infectious illness and there would have been more sterilising of the premises with sulphur candles.

1887 was, of course, a celebration year nation-wide—the Jubilee of Queen Victoria. It was not forgotten in Abriachan! On October 1st a treat is recorded thus: 'The School Board having granted a Jubilee gift of £5 to the school, the scholars, along with some of the parents and friends, on Thursday of this week had a trip by steamer to Fort Augustus, which they enjoyed immensely. School was kept today Saturday for Thursday'. Soon after this, on the 21st of the month, we read: 'The School Board Officer called on the most of the parents this week and told them distinctly that the Board was determined to prosecute all those who did not keep their children at school'. There were certainly instances of parents being fined for the children's absences. The teacher was doing his best to help. In September of the following year he says: 'opened school today at the request of some of the parents, as the harvest is so very late this year...better to give a fortnight or so again when the harvest comes on'. The parents are having their say and pointing out their priorities and the teacher is trying to co-operate.

January 25th 1889 has an important entry. It reads: 'Opened a night school on Monday of this week for grown-up boys and girls. The attendance is good and they are very diligent at their work, which is reading, writing, arithmetic, singing by the notes at the close. Hours from 7 till 9'. This report makes one wonder what the boys and girls did in their younger days at school! It was good that they had a chance to make up for lost time and that they ended their evening with song. This was typical of the teacher, Mr Mackay.

The entry for February 1st states 'D. Mackenzie, John Shaw, Monitor, and John Macdonald understand Euclid wonderfully well' yet on February 22nd an Inspector reports 'If better results are not produced by next inspection a reduction of grant may be made. It should be noted that special allowance has been made for the peculiar circumstances of the district'. Could it have been that the 'lads o' pairts' were outshining their less able contemporaries?

May 3rd brings a sad note—'Catherine Macmillan died from diphtheria this week and as the house is so close to the road from Caiplich the children from that district are afraid to come to school'. The peoples' great fear of infection probably originated in the time, not long past for them, when cholera reached epidemic proportions and caused many deaths. Families evicted from their homes all over the Highlands would congregate in villages and towns, hoping for shelter and perhaps work, and living in appalling conditions of squalor. They succumbed to diseases of many kinds and the contamination spread.

On June 2nd of that year Mr McGillivray, teacher in Abriachan for many years, died. His widow lived on in the old schoolhouse for a considerable time, bringing up orphan children. One of them was still there in our early days in Caiplich. He had the croft, had married a neighbour's daughter and brought up a fine family of his own. There were books in the house, he played the fiddle and one of his daughters was a pianist. It was a sad day when they all left the place and this old link with the school was gone. We went to the displenishing sale, bought a peat spade which I like to think was probably used by Mr McGillivray himself, and joined the neighbours in farewells.

In 1890, on March 21st, it is recorded: 'Mary Anne Macrae is still absent and the reason given is want of boots. She lives at a very high and cold place in the direction of Glen Urquhart'. When the weather warmed up she would have come barefoot, in any case. Attendance continued to worry the authorities. On May 22nd next year 'Mr Cameron, Default Officer, visited the school and told the children, in both languages, that the Board are determined to summons defaulting parents at their next meeting'. Is there a lesson here for parents of today?

In 1892 an important step was taken in the direction of looking on education as an essential social service. The payment of school fees was abolished. On 8th July there was a visit by the School Board members, 'a very pleasant one to the children and parents, a number of the latter having been present all the time'. In November we hear 'Wednesday, Thursday and Friday have been given for the lifting of the potatoes, by order of the school Board'. From these two entries it would appear that parents and Board are trying to co-operate. On December 30th 'Attendance was good, except today when some of them were sent to Inverness for the New Year messages'.

In 1893 on February 24th, 'By order of the County Council Dr McFadyen, Inverness, vaccinated 30 of the scholars today'. Here we have more evidence of social concern for the health and welfare of the children as well as the training of their minds. In that summer 'Three handsome books are to be given as prizes to three most deserving pupils by London, Inverness, Ross and Tain Association'. Next year was received 'A copy of scheme for Gaelic as a specific subject which is filed in the Portfolio'. One hoped it didn't stay in there too long! In April of the next year: 'The Hon. Mrs Baillie of Dochfour visited the school. She started a knitting class of grown-up girls, herself supplying all the materials to make stockings for the Highland Industries Society. The girls are very interested in the work'. This was part of an attempt to provide some small means of employment for the women. In May and June the 'Feeing Market' in Inverness and Parliamentary Polling Day meant no school. The following March brought outbreaks of whooping cough and scarlet fever. The school had to be closed until it had been 'thoroughly disinfected, whitewashed and the wood all varnished'.

On the Queen's Jubilee day in 1897 the children were 'taken to Inverness in four carriages. They enjoyed the day immensely and were all home about 8pm. They also each received a commemorative cup'. That same year the Inspector's report states, sadly, 'A higher grant cannot be recommended until the habit of inaudible answering in the senior room is eradicated'. Next January Jessie Mackay, the teacher's daughter, took charge of the Infants' Department. From then on there was always a woman to see to the youngest children.

That the school kept in touch with many events of importance is shown in the entry of June 8th 1900: 'On Friday school from 10am-2pm. The children were then taken to the top of Benlie [a nearby hill] to celebrate the fall of Pretoria, which they all enjoyed very much'. In February 1901 we read: 'For the last three months the children were supplied with soup between 1 and 2pm, greatly appreciated'. Times were evidently not getting any easier and the authorities were reacting to circumstances. A few years later a member of the School Board was

The girls of Mr Campbell's school, about 1910. Notice the bare feet!

supplying the children with warm cocoa, which was also much appreciated. The entry for October 4th reads: 'The children take a special interest in the free-arm drawing on the walls of the schoolroom which have been specially painted for this purpose'. Next we read: 'Corporal David Whitelaw of the 78th, an old pupil of the school and who is on furlough for a few weeks, is giving the boys drill in which they are most interested'. The interest of the pupils seems to have been always uppermost in this teacher's mind. In 1906 the much-loved Mr Mackay retired. He was given a pension of £48 6s. Thereafter the entries in the Log Book are of a different kind, strictly factual, giving less of the picture of the community.

Mr Peter Campbell was the new teacher. He stayed seven years, then moved to a low-ground school, where perhaps he had fewer problems with attendance, Gaelic-speaking and so on. His two sons distinguished themselves academically, one becoming Medical Officer of Health for the county, the other a lecturer in Classics at Edinburgh University, whose classes I was privileged to attend. His Highland voice reading Horace I shall always remember. Little did I think I would come to live in the house where he grew up!

In 1907 a Mr Buchanan of the Band of Hope in Glasgow gave a lecture to the children on Alcohol, its Nature and Use. Their enjoyment of this meeting is not recorded! The following year the Government, continuing in its role as good provider, made medical inspection and the serving of meals to poorer children compulsory.

In 1909 the Log Book reports: 'For the further development of Nature Study, practical School Gardening is to be introduced forthwith'. This was to be the start of many years of work undertaken with varying degrees of enthusiasm by different teachers over the years. After the first three years, when the school roll was 116, with many hands to lighten the work, the garden was inspected by an official of the College of Agriculture. One wonders what he made of this plot carved out of the moor.

In 1913 the first non-Highland and non-Gaelic speaking headmaster was appointed. His salary was £125, plus £5 for cleaning the 'offices' and £5 for superannuation. He had the house and garden with rates and taxes paid. He was from Glasgow and had been teaching for a short time in the Western Isles. He at once started lessons in Phonetics, as he found 'reading and writing very unsatisfactory'. By the following year he was getting homework done in jotters. He also had all the children weighed and measured.

There is little record of the impact of the Great War on the school. Teachers' posts were to be kept open and their salaries safeguarded. Not till near the end is there mention of any 'war effort' by the children. In September 1918 a letter from Mr Morrison, the Inspector, urges the importance of bramble-gathering. Very soon 35 lbs were duly dispatched. Sphagnum moss was also gathered. It was used in dressings for wounds. That same year School Boards were ended, their function taken over by Education Authorities. This meant a great loss of personal touch in the supervision of the schools and was regretted by many.

The Inspector's Report of 17th March 1920 says, quite simply, 'Singing is of exceptional merit in all respects'. This is the first indication of the particular achievement of this particular teacher, the superb training of the children in choral singing. He provided the accompaniment, with only a tuning fork, and his Highland assistant would see that the Gaelic wording was correct. The headmaster clearly recognised that the natural, inherited talent of the children had only to be discovered and a golden sound would emanate. And so it did. On September 24th of that year we read: 'Headmaster off duty on Tuesday, Wednesday, Thursday and Friday of this week attending the Mod in Oban with a junior choir'. In June 1928 the School Choir won the Craigmonie Trophy offered to Gaelic Junior Choirs and stood second among the Rural English Choirs at the Festival. In September they went to Fort William and got first prize for Choral Singing. Later that year they

Abriachan School Gaelic Choir

gave a concert in the Town Hall in Inverness, but were disqualified in one Trophy competition 'because the percentage of Gaelic speakers was below requirements'. This seems strange indeed, but shows how English was permeating the children's lives. Also, there were probably several 'boarded-out' children in the choir who had no Gaelic. Thereafter, we read that 'the timetable was to be re-arranged to allow 2 periods of Gaelic of ³/₄ hour each in the Senior Division. Other periods amounting to 2 hours to be spent with junior classes'. This meant a welcome revival of Gaelic. The following year the choir attended the Music Festival in Inverness and retained the Craigmonie Trophy for the third time. Eventually, they were to keep it six times and to secure the highest marks among sixteen school choirs. Their fame spread far and wide, and is remembered today.

In 1929 a shelter in the playground, for which parents of children who could not get home at dinner-time had been asking for several years, was at last completed. In January of the following year a dramatic entry records the 'sinking of the gallery in the classroom'. The result of this is left to the imagination! At that same time two boys reported their caps missing from the pegs in the cloakroom. Work had been going on at the water pipes and the cesspool. Eventually the caps were found—in the cesspool! Thereafter the headmaster demanded a fence round this unsavoury area.

In March 1932 there is the first record of a visit by Nurse Cran. Over the following years her visits became frequent and welcome. The state was continuing its job of providing welfare and the headmaster of the time certainly kept it and its agents on their toes! He was an innovator, and by dint of quite a bit of blustering he got things done. By pointing out the health risks of having 100 children using dry closets (which he objected to having to empty!) he persuaded the authorities to install flush cisterns. He agitated for the introduction of the telephone. On November 25th 1925 it was recorded: 'the local telephone office opened today and one of the children engaged the Town Clerk in conversation'. He insisted on better measures to prevent marauding sheep and roe deer from damaging vegetable crops in the garden. This meant putting up wire netting along the top of the wall. Some of it is still there. He got an extra classroom by partitioning the main room and got an extra teacher appointed.

In his personal life there were innovations, too. He had a bathroom installed in the house and he was the first person in the area to acquire a motor car. Many a time he sent the children scattering as he motored up the hill in his old Morris. Driving tests were not required at that time and red flags had gone out! The acquisition of the car meant that the pony which had pulled the trap to take his wife the ten miles to town could be put out to grass and a boy was no longer needed to walk at its head!

In 1932, on September 21st, the Log Book records: 'The centenary of Sir Walter Scott was observed by closing the school for one afternoon. Lessons were given appropriate to the occasion'. This shows, I think, the calibre of this teacher, who was, about this time, attending meetings of the Educational Institute of Scotland in Edinburgh.

After his retiral in 1935 and the death of his wife, he lived as a recluse in an isolated house on the hill road to Glenconvinth. The young people from Mrs Maclean's were in the habit of getting groceries for him from the van. He was still here when we came to live in the area. We were reluctant to visit him as we thought he would not welcome intrusion by strangers. Then, when we were on the point of venturing to make his acquaintance, we heard that he had died. His only daughter, also a teacher, made the arrangements for his burial in the nearby ground at Glenconvinth, where many Abriachan people lie. She took away all she wanted from the house and died herself a few years later. A family moved into the house and set about clearing the rooms. Bonfire flames were soon leaping into the evening sky. Knowing our interest in books they asked if we would care to save some of

Abriachan children at the 'Tattie Howking', 1943

them from the flames. We were over at the double! It was then that we realised what must have been the quality of the man's mind. There was a piano. There were books on every kind of subject—literature, the classics, art, music, crafts. We filled pillow-cases and staggered home under the weight of the tomes. Only then did we realise what his life must have been, isolated as he was, intellectually as well as physically.

The next headmaster was a very keen gardener. Two years after his appointment the Inspector's report goes like this: 'the headmaster here has transformed the garden into something very pleasing and deserves very great credit. With the help of the pupils the following improvements have been carried out: flower-plots, herbaceous border, lawn, rockery, crazy paving, hedges, rustic frame with roses, all carefully planned and neatly executed. The productive side is also included and the education aspect kept in view'. Alas, in subsequent years many of the attractive features created by this teacher were neglected as short-term tenants came and went. We have tried to rescue some of them.

In September 1939, as the Second World War was beginning, the school was closed for ten days. It was thought evacuated children might be coming, but this was not the case. In December the school won a Challenge Cup for gardening. The headmaster arranged lectures on bee-keeping for the boys. He kept goats and chickens and set a great example to others trying to help the war effort. Eventually he went to a bigger school not far away.

The school roll had fallen to about 45 when the next teacher took charge. The following year, as the war ended, an Act was passed which aimed to give children an education 'appropriate to the age, ability and aptitude' of the pupils. It also aimed to widen the scale of its provision of social welfare. The school leaving age was raised to 15. In Abriachan a canteen was opened for the service of school meals and over the following years, in spite of the decrease in the number of pupils, plans went ahead to erect a new building at the top of the playground so as to make the school into a Junior Secondary establishment. But nothing could stop the decline in the number of pupils.

By 1950 the school was reduced to one-teacher level, with its first headmistress in charge. There were 15 pupils on the roll. The idea of conversion to Junior Secondary status was given up. The equipment was removed from the classroom. In spite of a still falling number in school, electricity, which was coming to the whole area, was installed in the schoolhouse and the classrooms. Finally, in 1958, the school closed, as we have seen. It must have been a sad day for Miss Fraser to see the school close, the school where she had been a pupil, a pupil-teacher, then head. Her sister, too, had been a fellow-pupil and her forebears had attended the old school over the road. She continued teaching in other schools, before retiring and settling in Inverness. She came out many times to see us, always ready to help with our researches into the story of Abriachan, giving us many photographs and answering our many queries.

Chapter
Fourteen

The display of the Log Book extracts, together with a list of teachers, records of pupils and photographs of school groups taken at various times proved to be of great interest, especially to former residents of the area. In due course the improvements at the croft house, the publication of the booklet and the display of artefacts in the hall earned a further accolade from the authorities and an ornamental shield.

As news of the collection spread many interested people would come to visit. We had to restrict the opening hours and days so as to be able to cope with the situation. My husband was intensely interested in all aspects of the project and would often talk to the boys about old methods of construction and point out to them the remains of an old cruck-framed roof in a ruined building nearby, where the beams were held together with wooden pegs. Sometimes he would have to rush from the hall to the Post Office as a small queue of pensioners began to form at the schoolhouse door!

Our visitors were all people after our own hearts—people who would pick up a horn spoon or a chisel, turn it over and over, close to the face, smile, perhaps sigh a little and say, 'Aye, many's the time I've used that. I must bring you an adze. I have one out in the shed, I'm sure. I'll be along, maybe next week'. So it was that the collection slowly grew and grew. The things brought in were lovingly restored and labelled. Some were simple gifts, some on loan. Always it was understood that they would be returned if their owner so wished. Occasionally we managed to go to farm or croft sales to buy what we could afford. We still wandered round abandoned places and ruined the underparts of the van transporting cart wheels and, once, a stone roller!

One summer a party of French scouts arrived, without warning, pitching their tents in the field over the road. A thunderstorm, with torrential rain, greeted their arrival. We opened up the school, lit a fire in the grate and let them stay there till they were warm and dry. They were amazed to be welcomed in French and so thankful for the hospitality that they asked to be allowed to help in some way. The offer was gladly accepted and they put in a good day's work cutting weeds at the old graveyard at Kilianan. We became firm friends and they returned the following year to help again. On their last evening, they sang and played for us. It was good to hear the old schoolroom filled with the sound of French music and song. They had all heard of 'Marie Stuart' and her sad life. We told them of the affinity of the Highlands with France, of the many Jacobites who had fled there, of the clan chiefs who sent their sons to be schooled there and of the Auld Alliance which went back hundreds of years. They proudly displayed the tartan 'bunnets' they bought on their next day off, in Inverness!

Another year some Swiss scouts arrived. In return for permission to camp they, too, insisted on helping and did some good work in the garden of the croft house. The enthusiasm of both French and Swiss scouts was quite an inspiration and continued contact with them gave us a real link with Europe.

Very soon word got round the schools in Inverness and beyond that the Museum and the croft house were ready to receive visitors. Their educational potential was being recognised and assessed. Teachers would come out to look round, then, back in school, they would prepare the way for the children, perhaps make out sheets with basic questions for quickly pencilled answers. The children would certainly make a day of it, thrilled with everything they saw—except the loos in the playground! A picnic lunch and a walk, if there was time, would follow. Next day there would be a follow-up in class and the writing of a thank-you letter, saying what they had most enjoyed and why.

We enjoyed these visits. The children had a natural friendliness, we found. It seemed to shine out of them, especially on a fine summer day. They were mostly town children, the country an almost undiscovered wonderland. I would sometimes accompany them a little way up to the road to where the wild raspberries grew.

'Can you eat yon, Miss?'

One was always 'Miss', no matter what one's age or marital status.

'You can. You try.'

'Mmm...they're good.'

A friend comes up.

'I wouldn't. There's a spider on mine.'

She would only have seen nice clean rasps in tidy punnets! We sometimes wondered what the children really made of coming from their shiny houses, their shiny school, in their big shiny bus to see these old tools and cooking pots and implements that belonged to what must have seemed like another age. They liked the fact that nothing was out of reach, in a glass case. Everything could be inspected at close quarters, handled, picked up. And, amazingly, nothing got broken!

I remember one small boy, a quiet little fellow, picking up a small plane from among the joiners' tools. His face suddenly lit up.

'I mind—my grand-dad had one of those. He used to make...'

Suddenly overcome with shyness, he put it carefully back. As he moved on I could detect a touch of pride, of new assurance, in his walk. Was he thinking, 'Grandad's tools...in a museum? He must have been someone. Maybe...I'm someone?' Could he have got out of his visit something that formal education can't seem to give—a sense of his own identity? I think it's possible. He might have. I hope so.

Many of the children who came out in groups had read, in school, the story of 'The Kelpie's Pearls'. This is set in Abriachan. The author, Molly Hunter, lived here for a while. I remember her coming up, with her young son, to visit us, when we would discuss writing projects and ideas. She has since, of course, written many highly-regarded books and the 'Kelpie' has become a classic. After a close look, with the children, at the pots, the girdle, the kettle, the flat irons which old Morag of the story would have used I would point out the place where her house had been, the pool where the kelpie lived, the way down to the big loch and the one over the hill to Kiltarlity. Their eyes would widen as the story came so very much alive for them.

Members of various societies came to visit, too. Field Clubs, the National Trust. These learned visitors all contributed their valued share of knowledge and expertise, for which we were always grateful. The Inverness Field Club had been founded in 1875 after a memorable visit to Abriachan to study the geology of the area. Professor Young, of Glasgow University, had given three lectures on the geology of Scotland in Inverness. Thereafter, as recorded in the first volume of the Transactions of the Field Club, on 6th November 1875, a 'small party of seven, including Dr Young, set out in an omnibus—four inside and three perched on the box, to survey as much of the country as the mist left exposed to view'. At Abriachan the party examined the granite quarry, which 'yields a fine reddish stone, now frequently used for monuments'.

On their return home the interested parties resolved to constitute a society which would organise lectures in the winter months and outings in the summer, to 'seek and reveal' things of interest. A lively interest in Abriachan has been maintained through the years and several further visits made. Careful research and preparation are always undertaken by the leader of the group. Local people are always asked to contribute their knowledge and experience and many happy contacts have been established.

One year a visit was made to Craig-na-Uamh (the rock of the caves), which is 16¹/₂ feet high and 31¹/₂ feet long. Outside is a large boulder called Clach-na-Fion (stone of the Fingalians). Place-names give so many clues to history. It is said that Deirdre and her lover stayed for a time on a hill on the opposite side of Loch Ness at Dun Deardl. The cave at Craig-na-Uamh was said to be of a size to 'shelter forty sheep or goats on a stormy night'. Smugglers hid their bags of malt here. There were many cunning smugglers, who devised many cunning ways to outwit the gaugers, who were forever on their trail, sometimes sailing up and down the loch looking for tell-tale smoke from the distillers' fires. But some bothies were hidden underground and distilling could be carried on in broad daylight with fires of burnt heather or juniper, which give a smokeless fuel.

On 5th June 1886, during an outing to the area, there was much discussion about the derivation of the name Abriachan. Many theories have been put forward. It seems that the most likely origin is: Aber-riach-an—that is, the confluence of the speckled stream. The water from the hill burns meets the waters of Loch Ness after a series of magnificent waterfalls which are 'speckled' when the sun shines on the underlying granite and whinstone.

More stories about the big cave had been collected by the leader of the expedition, one concerning a notorious cattle-lifter, one Samuel Cameron, who sought shelter there when under threat of death. Out hunting one day, the Sheriff of Inverness came on him in the cave. Cameron at once threatened the intruder with his pistol, and, on learning who he was, shouted, 'Declare me a free man at the Cross of Inverness or I shoot you dead.' In this way he obtained his pardon and went on to live a sober life and to raise a large family.

On the loch shore below this famous 'Robber's Cave' were caves containing stalactites and stalagmites, which are still marked on some tourist maps. Sadly, they were demolished during road-widening operations in the 1930s. Children on their way to church at Bona, along the loch shore, would have had their first lessons in geology sheltering in these magical places. Travelling people—the 'summer walkers' as they were known—would shelter there too.

These 'summer walkers' of last century were mostly honest people living hard lives with quite strict codes of behaviour. Even forty years ago I remember a group of Stewarts who would camp at the roadside every year in Maytime. They were tin-smiths and the pans I bought from them lasted for years. One evening we would hear the scrape of a fiddle and next morning they would be gone. Many were descendants of those who had taken to the heather after Culloden and had never gone back to a settled life. Mostly they were made welcome during their brief stays. They brought news of other places, other happenings, in the days before radio and the easy circulation of newspapers. Sometimes a lone walker would appear, on his way over hill-tracks known to few to the west coast or the islands. He would get his bowl of brose or porridge and oatcakes for his pocket and be sent on his way with 'See you next year!' and a parting wave.

These people had a life-style and a culture all their own. 'Living off the land' came naturally to them, when there were fish to be 'guddled' in the burns, rabbit and hare to be despatched swiftly with a well-aimed stone, berries and nuts in season and all the summer plants to flavour the stew. Thyme made a healthy infusion and heather saw to many needs. It made a springy bed, a sparky fire, a quick hot drink and a long, cool, delicately flavoured thirst-quencher as ale. It figured in their crafts, too—small, tightly-bound sprigs of dried stalks making excellent pot-scrubbers. Clothes pegs of split birch twigs, baskets and creels of willow-wands—these would have won design awards for useful, environmentally friendly objects in today's age! Such skills are lost now as plastic and mass production take over the world of manufacture. Seasonal work can hardly be obtained these days, for machines cut out the need for 'hands'.

Story-telling, the singing of traditional songs and ballads, which was the customary way of passing the evenings and the winter days, these are going, as the radio blares out entertainment at all hours.

'The children get more schooling now,' I said to one traveller who has been calling at the door for years, selling mats, towels, needles and thread these days, in the style of the 'colporteurs'.

'Aye, they can read the paper and write their name and...'

'And add up the money at the end o' the day,' her husband chips in—'but they canna tell a horse fae a pony, nor light a fire at the roadside, nor find gulls' eggs for their breakfast. See me? I canna read nor write, but I can live the way I want. And they could, if they would learn.'

'I know what you mean.'

I think of the songs and stories being lost, too, as this old form of native education goes. We share a cup of morning tea and I wish them well 'till next year'. The children are at the gate, bright-eyed and sun-burnt, on their summer trek. I wonder about school and those 'shades of the prison-house'...

The Inverness Field Club outings to Abriachan brought the place alive for many people. In 1975, to mark the centenary of the founding of the club, I was privileged to give a talk, illustrated with slides, on the history of the area, from the earliest times. This was followed by an outing, one September day, to look at the various places of interest. We walked over the site of the prehistoric settlement on the hillside, went to see a smuggling bothy on the far shore of the little loch and looked at the cruck beams in one of the earliest houses. The flora and fauna were studied, too. A heron was fishing the loch. Buzzards were calling overhead, roe scampering through the birches. On the way home plastic bags were filled with brambles and various kinds of de-lectable mushroom.

On another occasion the graveyard at Kilianan was explored. It was not difficult to see, in the mind's eye, the early Columban settle-ment, the monks busy at their tasks and the boys coming to follow their teachings.

As time went by friends contributed many items of interest to our museum. One, a geologist, made up a collection of local minerals. Another, an artist, mounted a display board showing how lichens made different coloured dyes for wool. This interest we found most helpful and inspiring.

One day, in summer, a young scientist from Aberdeen University turned up at the door.

'I heard of the Museum here. May I see it?'

'Of course.'

She looked at everything with intense interest.

'I'm so pleased to be here. You see...my great, great, great, I forget how many greats, grandfather was headmaster in the school here.'

'He was? What was his name?'

'Lachlan Maclachlan. You've heard of him?'

'I have. Indeed I have. He was very well known. In fact, he was remembered, or his name was, until quite recently, by the old people.'

'That's good. I'd like to give something in his memory. I'll leave the money with you. Let me know what you decide to get.'

'That's a wonderful idea.'

'Lachlan Maclachlan'—the name had always had magical connota-tions. We had read about the man. He had become much more than a ghost-like figure. We had heard about his descendants and now we had met one. He had come here in 1776, somewhat reluctantly, as he had heard that the people were wild and addicted to smuggling. The making of the illicit dram was a common practice in many parts of the Highlands. It was a particularly strong brew and much favoured by many. Some of it was sold in order to pay the ever-increasing rents. Some of it was, inevitably, consumed locally. The Abriachan area was exceptionally suitable for the enterprise. The water was plentiful and pure, there were many hiding-places on the steep slopes, access by the gaugers was not easy and there was juniper, which gave a smokeless fire. The people became very clever at outwitting anyone who tried to curb their activities. Some of them also indulged in gambling at cards, a game perhaps learned through service at the 'Big House', where such things took place. The main sport was shinty. Their love of the game was such that matches often took place on the Sabbath.

Lachlan Maclachlan, whose duties as schoolmaster included catechising and sometimes preaching, as well as teaching, went warily about his mission among the people. He even agreed to join in their Sabbath game if they would agree to play fair and to come to his religious meeting afterwards. I think he was well ahead of his time in many respects. The people agreed with his proposal and kept their word, so real contact was made.

Lachlan was a poet, too. He used this gift to write satires on gambling, drunkenness and other vices. The people appreciated this and responded in large measure. Soon he became highly regarded and was known as 'Mr Lachlan'. Descendants of his were famed Gaelic scholars and ministers of religion in Edinburgh and elsewhere. So...how to keep his memory alive?

We decided to buy a seat which people could rest on as they looked across to the fields and hills that Lachlan must have looked at so often. The remnants of his little school remain, just a tumble of stones now, some of them made into a wayside dyke. But the building served its purpose until 1875, when the big school was put up. Mr Lachlan would have had to make do with a very primitive schoolroom, about 36 feet by 16, with an earth floor, small windows, a thatched roof, often leaking, and a fire in the middle, for which the children brought peats. For furnishings—a table for himself and forms for the pupils, but no desks and few books. This school had been established by the Scottish Society for the Propagation of Christian Knowledge. In the records, against Mr Maclachan's name, the comment 'wants books' occurs regularly. One can imagine the scholarly man's frustration at the lack of this basic work tool. Perhaps things have not changed much 200 years on!

IN MEMORY OF

LACHLAN MACLACHLAN

SCHOOLMASTER AT ABRIACHAN
1776 – 1798

DEAN SUIDHE

The memorial plaque for Lachlan Maclachlan

As for his house, it probably consisted of not more than two rooms, of primitive structure, attached to the school.

We bought a teak seat and a plaque for Mr Maclachlan's name. In order to get the dates of his schoolmastering accurate, we wrote to the Church of Scotland Offices in Edinburgh. They referred us to the Scottish Record Office, where the records of the S.S.P.C.K. are kept. The people there we found most cooperative. They sent us, not only Mr Lachlan's dates, but the dates of all the other schoolmasters of the Society who had served in Abriachan and also accounts of visits by Inspectors over several years, from the early nineteenth century. These we found of great interest. They give a picture of schooling as part of the life of the community. We hear of times of hardship and illness, of catechising and religious meetings, of the children who have learnt to read reading the scriptures to their parents in their homes, especially during the winter when they could seldom go to the Parish Church, which was ten miles distant.

Mr Lachlan's wife taught sewing and knitting to women and girls, in an evening class. It is not recorded whether she was paid. Her husband's salary was £10 a year. This was more or less the equivalent of a labourer's pay. He would also have received a small sum from the

Heritors, small emoluments for acting as Catechist, perhaps as Registrar and so on, and fees paid by the parents. These varied from place to place. The year was divided into four quarters—Lammas, Hallowmas, Candlemas, and Beltane. Fees were paid by the quarter, typically:

1s 6d a quarter for reading
2s 6d a quarter for reading and writing
2s 6d a quarter for the 3 Rs
2s 6d a quarter extra for Latin

Some parents could only afford to send their children to school a quarter at a time.

In most places the master's salary was augmented by a charge for cock-fighting, which took place in the schoolroom. There is no record of fights in Abriachan but they probably took place. They were held on Shrove Tuesday. Parents and very often the minister would attend. Defeated birds became the perquisites of the schoolmaster and were no doubt a welcome addition to his larder. Hugh Miller, in his book *My Schools and Schoolmasters*, gives an account of the fights in his day. He says:

The school...had its yearly cockfight, preceded by two holidays and a half during which the boys occupied themselves in collecting and bringing up their cocks and such always was the array of fighting birds mustered on the occasion that the day of the festival, from morning till night, used to be spent in fighting out the battle. For weeks after it had passed the school floor would continue to retain its deeply stained blotches of blood...the yearly fight was a relic of a barbarous age. Every boy had to pay the master two pence per head for leave to bring his birds to the fight.

Miller goes on to say that he never attended a fight. This is perhaps an interesting glimpse of his true nature. He was writing of what took place in the early years of the nineteenth century. He describes his school thus: 'The building in which we met was a low, long straw-thatched cottage, open from gable to gable with a mud floor below and an unlathed roof above'. This sounds very like Mr Maclachlan's school.

The teaching in schools run by the S.S.P.C.K. was supposed to be in English, but many times Gaelic had to be used as the children really understood no other language and would be repeating words with no

understanding of their meaning. The hours of attendance were long—
from February to October the school was open every weekday from 7
to 11 am and 1 to 5 pm. For the rest of the year the hours were 8 to 12
am and 1 to 3 or 4 pm. In late summer there were three weeks of
holiday (the 'harvest play'). Christmas or New Year breaks were very
short and Easter was barely recognised.

The children's lives were thus filled with long hours of schooling,
largely dispensed in an alien tongue, with alien ideas having to pre-
dominate. Mr Maclachlan would surely have tried his utmost to keep
things in some sort of proportion, but his efforts would have been
restricted by his commitment to the Society. It must have been galling
for a man of his intellectual calibre and with so close an affinity with
his charges, to have to witness the slow erosion of their culture, in
what must surely have been the start of a kind of ethnic cleansing. His
daughter Helen, as we have seen, married a local Macdonald; another
daughter, Janet, married a later teacher in Abriachan and their son
became a teacher in the area. A grandson was the Rev. Dr Thomas
Mclachlan (1816-86), one of the foremost Gaelic scholars of his time
and a Moderator of the Free Church. The struggle to preserve the old
Highland heritage would have gone on valiantly in hands such as these.

Chapter Fifteen

About this time I began to wonder whether I could risk giving up my 'day job' so as to be able to be full time 'at home'. Home was the centre of much activity, people coming and going to the Post Office, the Project sites, naturalists, archaeologists passing by, young friends, old friends, relatives turning up to stay. This activity we enjoyed immensely, of course. But it did demand a toll. After days and evenings of discussion it was decided that I would take what we now call 'early retirement' and retreat to the home front. I found myself, of course, busier than ever! Breakfast was a snatched cup of tea taken standing at the toaster, lunch a sandwich munched walking round the garden, looking at the jobs to be done. But the evenings were relaxed, with no papers to correct, mark sheets to add up, reports to be written or lessons prepared. I missed the daily contact with the school. I remembered my father's saying: 'Being with the young keeps you young'. Gradually things settled down. I taught an evening class at the College for several winters and very much enjoyed working with a group of interested adults. I was also doing scripts for schools radio and—there was the garden. We grew most of the vegetables we needed by dint of ingenious methods of protecting seedlings, including jam jars and plastic bottles. We had Bridget the goat, our chickens and five hives of bees. So basic sustenance was assured.

Helen, after getting her degree and teaching English abroad for a year, had married and was living on a small farm, almost a croft, some twenty miles away. She was milking a Jersey cow, tending calves and chickens and growing vegetables of a size we never managed to achieve in the heights. In due course, two small girls arrived. They did much to lighten the next few years, when Jim's health was failing, and at five and six years old they smoothed the way for him to the Elysian fields.

I knew where he would like to be remembered. In the little burying-ground at Kilianan we had worked together so often, cutting weeds, planting bulbs. We had come to feel we would recognise the people lying there. A few had carved and inscribed memorial head-stones showing lineage and identity. For most there was a rough-hewn piece of granite, decorated only with moss and lichen.

It is said there was a chapel there long after the monks had gone, and latterly it had been a preaching-site. St Columba's font remains and the sanctuary stone still stands. Not far away, in the shelter of a stand of tall pines, is the place where a small tinker child was buried, her parents not seeking the comfort of a Christian burial. Though the nearby road is busy, now, with traffic, there is still the aura of peace about the place.

For weeks I searched for a stone, along the loch shore, among the crags, up in the hill-top quarry which had yielded building material. To find a piece of the right size and shape and then to think out means of transport, these were the problems. At last I found it—a beautiful piece of rose-red granite, lying on the ground at the entrance to an old steading. It had evidently formed the lintel of the doorway. And it would have come from the hill-top quarry, as this was one of the high crofts. The owner of the property more than kindly allowed me to have it and another neighbour, who was working with a digger in the area, transported it willingly to a sculptor for inscription. It was arranged that it could be placed in a quiet corner of the graveyard, where the snowdrops come, even in the snow. We scattered the ashes round the foot of the stone, some round the sanctuary stone, and planted bulbs of all the companion flowers of spring. We knew Jim would have been happy in the company of the crofters, the stone-mason, the shoemaker, the Norwegian princess, all the others who share his resting place.

It was decided, then, that I would keep on working the Post Office, as otherwise, they said, it would be closed. It is a very small office, some say about the smallest in the country, and not a very busy one, as the commuters tend to buy stamps or Postal Orders when out shopping at lunch-time in the town. It still has a purpose, though, as the one focal point, now when there is no school, no church and no shop. The Postman can report any illness or accident he may have encountered on his round and prompt action can be taken, neighbours alerted, help summoned on the phone. There is also a small branch of the Public Library squeezed into an old bookcase in the porch, beside the office equipment, the scales, the leaflets and so on. This collection of books is prized by the few remaining readers, especially when snow or ice make the journey to town hazardous.

My duties in the Post Office kept me tied to the house every morning

Miss Fraser and the pupils of the school in 1952

and for a short spell in late afternoon. This meant that escorting people to the Museum had to be fitted in between afternoon hours in the
garden. Somehow, it was managed. Parties coming by appointment
could be coped with reasonably easily. When a small, eager group arrived, just as I had started to single lettuces on a glorious summer
afternoon, I had to struggle a welcoming smile as I kicked off my wel-
lies, washed my hands at the water-butt, smoothed my hair, found the
keys and began my 'spiel'. The interest and appreciation in the faces
and voices of the folk as they packed into their cars for 'off' was certainly rewarding.

There were many happy occasions, too, when I would hear a creak
as the garden gate swung open, approaching footsteps, a murmur of
voices and would look up to find two or three people 'of a certain age'
gazing at the house, at the school, obviously re-orienting themselves
after a long absence.

'We were at school here' one of them would say. 'I remember yon
high windows. We could never see out. But the ivy would come in!'

'As it does today' I say, looking up. 'I have a grandson who's better
than I am at climbing ladders now. He'll be here one day soon to cut it
back. Would you like to see inside the school?'

'Oh yes, please.'

They wander round, looking into every corner, in silence. Then the real remembering starts.

'That was the infants' room' the oldest visitor says. 'That's where I started. I mind it like yesterday. And the teacher was good to us. She would take us out on a summer's day for a walk down the road and a lesson sitting under the bushes.'

'Aye. And on the Sabbath she would have us to her house to sing hymns and give us sweeties afterwards...' her friend remembers.

'But the master. In the big room. That was a different kettle o' fish.' The man in the party has his own memories.

'Well, he had to keep you laddies in order.'

'He did that. And it must have been some job when there were near a hundred o' us. We knew fine when to expect the worst—the days he came into school wi' his hat on. That was a bad sign. We'd try to hide the strap on those days, if ever his back was turned.'

'And he was daft about singing. I can see him now, wi' his tuning fork. And the skelp you got if you sang a wrong note.'

'But he made a good job of the choir.'

'He did. And all the prizes it won made the school famous.'

'And some boys got Latin and geometry. They were the brains.'

They were all reminiscing now, thoughtfully. I imagine a small, barefoot boy, a last-minute rip in his kilt held together by a safety-pin, trudging along the track from one of the high places, puzzling over the square on the hypotenuse or the use of the ablative case in a subordinate clause, as he swings his small bundle of tattered books to the rhythm of his stride. He would have been heading straight for a job in a bank or on the Highland Railway, so his parents hoped.

'And out of all those pupils, have you kept in touch with some?'

'With some, yes. But many went away to the war. Highlanders always did that, of course. There were doctors and teachers and engineers, aye, and ministers, too, among them. Education went into most of them, one way or another.'

'Your families belonged to Abriachan?'

'No. We were orphans. But we were all lodged with good people in good homes. So this is real home to us still.'

They were reluctant to leave the school premises.

'D'you mind if we take a wee walk round outside?'

'Of course not.'

'The shelter's there. I bet my initials are on the wall yet.'

'And the loos...' with a giggle, 'I hated having to go, with yon wee

Sculptured grave slab from Kilianan

slats on the door!'

'But we'd sometimes find some fallen apples off the tree up yonder. They were soor!'

'Come in for a cup of tea before you go...'

They wander off. Reminiscences such as these brought the place so vividly alive that sometimes I wondered if I was living in yesterday or today. Some days people would come from overseas, looking for the home of their ancestors. We could perhaps trace it from the name, then have to announce, sadly, that it was now no more than a heap of stones. Sometimes the information was so scant that it was impossible to recommend a visit to the library in Inverness, where there is a resident genealogist and much material on computer.

Interesting documents and photographs continued to arrive from people who seemed as glad to find a home for them as we were to provide that home. Photographs were always copied so that the originals could be returned to their owners, if they so wished. I particularly treasured the school groups and only wished the camera had been invented in the time of Lachlan Maclachlan and his scholars.

Glimpses of schooling in the not-too-distant past led me to try to reach back into the very earliest times. The people in these parts must have been among the most fortunate in the Highlands. They had the centre of learning established as early as the sixth century by Columba's missionaries at Kilianan, just down the road. Here, as we have seen, able boys would have been taught the elements of Latin grammar, some Greek and also to read and write in their native tongue, which was akin to Columba's own. They would have learnt husbandry, too, and some basic technical skills in the working of wood and metal. Another craft—the illumination of manuscripts—they would have learnt readily enough. From their Pictish ancestry they would have inherited the gift for working in stone. Embellishing parchment would have seemed a logical transfer of skill. Music and storytelling would have fed their imagination. Columba himself was a writer of no mean ability. He is said to have composed many 'lays', or tales of heroes. Wandering minstrels, too, would have provided history lessons in a very attractive form.

Sadly, many of these civilising influences would have been lost over succeeding centuries when Viking invasions and civil wars dominated peoples' lives. But as Christianity re-asserted itself and priories and abbeys were founded, notably one at Beauly, only some ten miles distant, teaching would have been available again for young men wishing to enter the church. Some less ambitious scholars were catered for also. They were known as 'scolacs' and earned their keep by doing manual work in addition to studying. Some well-known scholars taught in the Priory at Beauly and at the Abbey at Kinloss, a few miles down the coast.

As time went on and the value of education was recognised more and more fully, schools were established in towns such as Inverness, a place reasonably accessible to boys from Abriachan and to which all the secondary pupils of today go. There were also the 'Sang Schules', in which singing was of prime importance, this to ensure choral excellence at church services. The main schools, too, were church-oriented. They were known as 'Grammar' schools, the grammar being Latin grammar, as Latin was the language of the church and also an international language, used in teaching all over Europe. Scholars could wander happily from one University to another and often did. The Scots of Leyden, Paris and Rome may well have included young men from Abriachan.

By an Act of 1496, James IV made it incumbent on barons to send their sons to the Grammar Schools. He was keen to build up a body of educated men to run the establishment. This was the first Act of its kind—an Education Act—to be passed in Europe. In the Miscellany of the Spalding Club there is a reprint of the Rules and Statutes of the Ancient Grammar School of the city of Aberdeen. These would have applied in most of the pre-Reformation schools of the time. Life was not easy. The day started with prayers and at 7 the 'prescribed task' was begun. Those who failed in this would be punished 'by word or lash' by the preceptor. Thereafter lectures went on with an interval for breakfast and one for dinner at 12. From 2 to 4 there were more lectures and from 5 to 6 'disputations', followed by prayers. Pupils were able to speak in Latin, Greek, Hebrew, French or Irish (Gaelic), never in the 'common' tongue. Presumably this common tongue would have been a dialect form of English. This is interesting in view of later developments regarding the use of language. No gambling or dice-playing was allowed. There were many punishable offences, including 'wasting time when allowed to leave the room'. One can imagine boys from the hills, encouraged to attend a school such as this one, finding the going difficult. Yet many Highland chiefs sent their sons to the Grammar Schools.

With the Reformation came a renewed interest in the spread of learning, possibly partly as a means of propagating the new ideas in religion. Looking at this period, I find John Knox appearing in a new light. He and his coterie, known as the 'Six Johns', in 1560 drew up a treatise called the 'First Book of Discipline'. These Johns were really men of vision, who regarded education as the right of all children, girls as well as boys. The rich were to be compelled to send their children to school and 'the children of the poore most be supportit and sustenit on the charge of the Churche till tryell be taken whether the spirit of docilitie be fund in them or not', docilitie meaning the ability to undergo instruction. Knox must surely not have been without a (perhaps unconscious) sense of humour when he declares, somewhere in the treatise, 'God hath determined that his Church shall be taught, not be angellis but by men' and 'now cessaith to illuminat men miraculaslie'.

Knox would have wished to see a school in every parish. The parishes, of course, were enormous, some of them the size of a whole county of today. Many schools would have been needed to cater for even half the children. It was not until nearly a hundred years after Knox's time that a start was made, with an Act for the Founding of Schools. These early Parish Schools were set up in any available building, even a church, a barn or an inn. The masters, though poorly paid, were mostly men of sound learning, many hoping to become ministers of religion. The Heritors, as the landowners were known, were supposed to see to the setting-up of the schools. In some parts they complied in a satisfactory way, in others they did not. There is no record of a Parish School in Abriachan, though there were several in nearby Glen Urquhart. School life was hard for teachers and pupils alike, with long hours, few holidays and, for the master, scant reward. But there were times of enjoyment. At New Year great day-long shinty games were played, with few restrictions on the number of players or the size of the field of play. Sometimes the ball would land in the next parish and half the players with it. On Candlemas Day—2nd February—each pupil was supposed to bring a gift for the master, a kind of late Christmas present. The biggest event of the year, as we have seen, the cock-fight, was held on Shrove Tuesday. This somewhat barbaric activity was continued over the next some three hundred years.

Throughout the seventeenth century the Assembly of the Church made valiant attempts to ensure the establishment of schools, but without the cooperation of the Heritors this was an uphill task. Times were hard, there was much poverty and unrest, with Civil War raging in many parts. The Heritors themselves were not wealthy. The provision of proper buildings and the master's pay would have taxed their resources. It is likely that, in some cases, they were not too keen on having an educated tenantry. The illiterate were, perhaps, easier to control. The days of the clan as an extended family, under the patronage of the Chief, were beginning to disappear. The clan lands, becoming known as 'estates', had to be made to produce some sort of profit. As communication with the south was opening the Highland Heritors saw their counterparts there enjoying lives of comparative luxury, which they resolved to emulate.

Chapter Sixteen

The year 1696 marked a watershed in the story of education in the country. Two hundred years after James IV's Act, an Act of Parliament—'The Act of Settling Schools'—finally established the Parochial System, making it obligatory for Heritors to erect a school and provide for a teacher, with a threat of penalty for non-compliance. For many years, in the majority of Highland parishes, the Act was ignored. The chiefs sent their sons to the grammar schools of Inverness and other places. The sons of some true Jacobites were sent to school in France. In some cases the better-off hired a teacher to instruct their children privately. For the children of the poor there was no provision made.

The master was to have a salary, fees and 'perquisites'. The salary was 100 - 200 merks (£5 - £10). The minister had twenty times more. The fees were fixed by the Heritors, e.g. 5 shillings a quarter. The buildings were everywhere inadequate. One 'school' is described as consisting of one room, the master teaching at one end, his wife cooking at the other.

The running of the schools was to be undertaken by the Church Presbyteries. Some Heritors saw this kind of schooling, where the teaching was to be in English, as an assault on their native culture and an attempt to lessen their hereditary power.

Travellers from the south were beginning, at this time, to make their way into the more remote regions of the Highlands and to report back on the conditions in which they found the people living. Some of these reports no doubt spread fear and alarm among the citizens in the south. The thought of increasing numbers of uneducated and probably undisciplined young gave rise to feelings of unease.

Then, in 1701, in Edinburgh, a few private gentlemen met to institute a society for 'further promoting of Christian knowledge and the increase of piety and virtue within Scotland, especially in the Highlands and islands and remote corners thereof'. Members were to be

Protestant. Teachers were forbidden to teach in Latin (the language of the Catholic Church) or Gaelic, all instruction to be in plain English. One of the first schools of this Society, now known as the Scottish Society for the Propagation of Christian Knowledge, was set up in St Kilda in 1711, when there were 28 scholars. Some Society teachers ventured to America, to work among the 'Indians'. Their first Highland school, in the village now known as Fort Augustus, was a failure. The style of teaching, in English, for children whose language and cultural background was entirely Gaelic, was so disliked by the people that the establishment had to close after 18 months. Later, the Society relaxed its attitude to the prohibition of Gaelic in the schools. In 1767 a Gaelic translation of the New Testament was introduced.

There is no record of a school building in Abriachan, but the name of James Rhind appears in the annals of the Society as teacher there in 1766, at a salary of £6 a year. There were 9 girls and 25 boys on the register. Ten years later, when Lachlan Maclachlan was appointed, there were some 40 scholars on the roll. He had been teaching in other parts of the parish and had to be persuaded, by means of a 'peremptory letter', to take up the post in Abriachan. Once settled there, he made, as we have seen, a solid success of his time among the people. It was not an easy time in the country as a whole. Families were being evicted from their homes, to make way for sheep and sheep farmers, in what became known as the Clearances, when the Heritors were making 'improvements' on their estates. It is interesting to note that during Mr Lachlan's time Burns was writing valiantly and the French Revolution was taking place. News of these happenings would surely have reached his ears.

Schooling continued in Abriachan for close on two hundred years. During those years the names of 16 head teachers are recorded. Some stayed only three or four years. These were most likely men hoping for a more lucrative appointment, perhaps overseas, in India or wherever opportunities were opening up. Most stayed some ten or twelve years, the longest spells being those of Lachlan Maclachlan's 21 years and Donald Mackay's 22. These were people who clearly understood the way of life of a Highland community and, because of this, they received the affection and support of the people.

In some places the Parish Schools continued to exist along with those established by the S.S.P.C.K. Elsewhere, the establishment of a Society school gave the Heritor an excuse not to provide a Parish School. There were some disagreements between the two types of school over the methods of religious instruction. The Heritors, ever reluctant to heed directives from the south, allowed things to drift. In 1803, soon after Lachlan Maclachlan had ceased teaching and when John Fraser was headmaster, an Act was passed 'for making better provision for the Parochial schoolmasters and for making further regulations for the better government of the Parish schools'. The master's salary was to be raised, he was to have a house of at least two rooms, with a garden of at least ¹/₄ acre Scots. This valiant attempt to improve standards in education was prompted, at least in part, by the Napoleonic Wars, when it was feared that the soldiers were not sufficiently educated to meet the demands of modern warfare. In places where the Parish school was inadequate to provide education for the growing number of pupils, 'side' schools were set up, small establishments, often poorly housed, with unqualified teachers, to take the overflow.

During the early years of the nineteenth century Gaelic Societies were established, their aim being to support schools in the Highlands and Islands in which teaching would be in Gaelic, so that the children would be able to read the Bible in their native language. The teacher's salary would be modest as he took no fees, but he could rely on the people to provide his material needs of shelter and food. Sometimes a student was appointed who taught during his summer holidays and spent the winter studying.

No mention of any of these agencies to promote education occurs in the annals of Abriachan. After Mr Maclachlan's departure in 1797 the names of Lachlan Fraser and John Fraser appear in the records. They remained in charge for three years and thereafter John Fraser stayed in the post for a number of years. A report dated 1803 states that the number of scholars was 41 and that they were competent in reading the Bible in English and in Gaelic and also in repeating the Lord's Prayer, the Creed and the Ten Commandments and in answering the questions of the Shorter Catechism. So the Gaelic was clearly surviving here. The schoolmaster's wife had a 'thriving school of industry' going, teaching the girls spinning, sewing and knitting.

In the more remote areas of the Highlands, where there seemed little likelihood of a school of any kind being set up, families would join together to employ a student to teach their children, independently of any organisation. It is interesting to note that Robert Burns' father employed a tutor to teach his son Latin and Greek and a smattering of French, to supplement the teaching he must have had in school.

The population, at this time, was increasing, in spite of emigration, and there was a growing realisation that many children were receiving little or no education. In Inverness a 'Society for educating the poor in the Highlands' was started. In 1825 it sent out to every parish minister a questionnaire which he was to distribute to all the families asking the numbers who could read, whether they understood English or Gaelic best and the distance they were from the nearest school. The investigation found that half the inhabitants were unable to read and one third lived more than two miles from school. Many thousands lived more than five miles from school.

One day, during John Fraser's time in the school, a Mr Thomas Fraser, along with an elder, a tenant and some parents was visiting the school in this 'detached and isolated place' and was struck by the scarcity of books, particularly of Bibles and other religious books. He therefore wrote to the heritor, Sir James Grant, requesting him to obtain the necessary books from the Society so that the children could read the scriptures, at home, to their parents, who were mostly illiterate. It is likely this request was granted as Sir James was not an illiberal heritor.

In 1824, when 55 scholars are in attendance during winter an Inspector finds the master confined to bed and his son taking the lessons. The people express to him their concern over the master's illness, as they value his religious instruction, given with the approval of the parish minister (which was not always the case) as well as his teaching of their children. They also value his encouragement in their learning to read the Bible in Gaelic which they much prefer, as they hardly understand any other language. Teaching methods were clearly becoming more relaxed.

This report contains the first mention of a school in the neighbouring area of Caiplich, which it described as being one mile distant but separated by a hill 'impassable in winter'. In later years this school is described as being 'four miles distant'. In actual fact it is probably somewhere between the two, unless you're a crow! There were 40 scholars there at the time, with a young schoolmaster 'of apparently serious disposition'.

The next mention of this school is in a report of 1867, when Mr Lewis Robertson is named as teacher, with 25 pupils on the roll. Religious knowledge was very good and the Shorter Catechism excellent, the report says. Gaelic was often used in teaching, as the children did not understand English. There is no mention of a schoolhouse. Very likely the teacher, if he was a young man, would lodge with a family. From 1870 to 1873 Mr Archibald Maclean's name is on the register. He is still remembered as a legendary character by the few remaining native people of the area. After this it seems that the school may have been discontinued for a time, perhaps after the provision of the new school in Abriachan. It is next mentioned in the minutes of the School Board of the 11th April 1902 thus: 'The inhabitants of Caiplich...wanted a school as they are 4 miles from Abriachan school'. On 6th May of that year the minutes record: 'It is to be built. It is to have two rooms'. The parents were evidently making themselves heard and heeded. I can find no reference to the closing of this school. One wall still stands, tall and firm, though much of the stone has been removed from other parts, probably to repair dykes or houses. The perimeter of the playground is still visible and the well still flows. Legend has it that the sound of children singing can be clearly heard on a still day. One of Mr Robertson's hymns or of Mr Maclean's songs? A happy haunting, anyway.

In 1825 Mr Neil Maclean, a married man of 30, arrived to teach school in Abriachan. The population then was 300 and the language exclusively Gaelic. 84 scholars attended during the winter months. A new schoolhouse was built at this time, but Mr Maclean stayed only seven years, then went to teach in Lewis.

In 1833 Mr Donald Tolmie is in charge. He is well spoken of by the Inspector and by the people. On the day of inspection the scholars had been competing with four other schools for prizes given by the Celtic Society and had carried off the greater number of awards. Two years later, in 1835, another visit of inspection took place. Mr Tolmie was away at a funeral. They examined 'such of the classes as understood English' and were quite satisfied with what they found.

Mrs Fraser, widow of John Fraser, the teacher, who died in 1825, was still in charge of the 'female school' and was in the habit of making one girl read while the others were sewing or knitting. This was considered 'an exceedingly good plan' and was much approved of. Mr Tolmie eventually seceded to the Free Church after the disruption of 1843, and from 1846 to 1859 the register of teachers is blank. The people petitioned for his return, but the Society had strict rules. Seceders were considered to have disruptive tendencies. The school was probably taught by students or other volunteers, but there is no record of their names. The Free Church authorities were setting up schools of their own.

In 1838 another Act had been passed, in a further effort to 'Facilitate the Foundation and Endowment of additional schools in Scotland'. Under the terms of this Act the Government would provide the teacher's salary, while the heritors continued to maintain the school and schoolhouse. Still there was an ever-increasing demand for educational

The 'School Croft'

facilities. There were 'adventure' schools, small schools set up by private persons for their own benefit. These were often held in cramped conditions and taught by an elderly woman, the children sitting, along with her own family, round the fire. In one case it is recorded that a shoe-maker taught a group of boys to read, while plying his own trade. Doubtless they learnt to make shoes as well as to read!

For one year, 1859-60, a Mr Duncan Ferguson's name appears in the record of teachers in Abriachan. Then, in 1861, things are back to normal with the appointment of Mr Angus McGillivray, who was to remain at his post for 13 years. He had 45 pupils on the roll and was to be the last man to teach in the old building. It is described by an Inspector as 'sound but very rough'. Mrs McGillivray taught sewing in the same room used by her husband for his classes. In these cramped conditions reading and spelling yet achieved the comment 'good', though geography and arithmetic were only 'fair'. Copybooks are described as 'clean and carefully written'. Of singing there was none. Discipline was good and the school was considered a definite asset in the community. In a later report reading is described as 'fluent and careful' but 'the Gaelic accent which is marked renders it less intelligible than it might otherwise be'. Writing and arithmetic are pronounced only 'fair', though 'dictation and slate writing' are very good.

The school accommodations were by now in a 'state of great dilapidation'. Mr McGillivray must have had strange thoughts as he watched the great new school being built just over the road. He was no doubt glad to be retiring, to be escaping all the new rules and regulations coming in after the 1872 Education Act and to be retreating to his cosy house and his 'school croft'. All this—house, garden, croft and grazing—is still in existence today, the place being still known as the School Croft. It is, appropriately, occupied by a schoolmaster, a man genuinely interested in education, and his family.

During Mr McGillivray's time, in 1864, the Argyll Commission (named after its chairman) had been set up to investigate and report on the state of education over the whole country. It recommended an education rate, rigorous inspection, grants for much needed new buildings and a superannuation scheme to relieve teachers of worry over security in old age. These recommendations were reflected in the provisions of the 1872 Act.

Chapter
Seventeen

Many fruitful hours and days were spent delving into records, listening to stories, studying photographs till the tale of schooling in these hills became as real to us as the doings of day-to-day life. We could see the children coming down the high tracks, in summer sun and winter blizzard, hear the bell clanging to gather them into the playground, hear the buzz of learning and reciting lessons, the shouts and laughter at the dinner-play, the gruff tones of an over-wrought headmaster.

Meantime the present-day function of the school was changing with changing times. Over the next few years new burdens in the shape of massive amounts of paper-work, record-keeping, the design of teaching modules and so on, with changes in the patterns of the curriculum, weighed heavily on teachers everywhere. Less and less time was available for peripheral activities and eventually outings to Abriachan ceased altogether. Only in times of real crisis could help be called on from the 'technical' staff.

One such occurred one morning in May when a neighbour, making a call from the telephone box up the road, reported that the door of the croft house at Druim had been broken. I hurried to investigate. Sure enough, the old double door had been forced and part of it shattered. I went in. The bed had obviously been slept in, but nothing had been taken. It had obviously been a case of bed and no breakfast. I rang the High School and explained the urgency of getting a repair done. We couldn't afford a string of benighted tourists sleeping in the old box bed. The response was swift. Hammer and nails and some planks of wood restored the door.

Strangely enough, almost exactly a year later, on a beautiful morning in May, we found the same thing had happened again. The door was forced, the bed slept in, nothing was taken. I imagine the same wee man must have come wandering this way again, knowing he could depend on a good night's sleep in the house at Druim. Perhaps he or his forebears had lived there once? It was intriguing. But repairs were needed again. This time a local man, a skilled joiner, was available to help. He worked with care and concern and we drew breath once more. After that, I felt obliged to remove some of the things that future guests might one day feel like removing—the porridge bowls and horn spoons from the kitchen table, the tea-pot and the Gaelic Bible from the dresser. The following May I kept as strict a watch as possible on the house, but no traveller arrived.

Our next intruders were of a very different ilk. The bottom part of the side of the double door which had not been forced, and so not repaired, had been rotting. We knew it would have to be replaced eventually, but reckoned it would do for a time, as long as the lock was fast. For our intruders it opened the way to exciting possibilities. On my next visit to the house I noticed that the rotting portion at the foot of the door had been enlarged. Intrigued, I went inside. There was a scuffling and the sound of a hurried scamper up the ladder-like stairway to the loft. I crept up cautiously and managed to glimpse a pair of very bright eyes staring, or rather glaring, with more than a

The pine marten

touch of menace. A small brown body, with a flicker of orange, vanished into a dark corner and all was quiet. Unmistakably a pine marten. I had seen one before, with a baleful look in the same bright eyes, as it was forced to abandon a marauding attack on a bevy of hens. Beautiful creatures they are, but fearless, with a vicious touch to their natures. I went down. There was no further sound. In the two main rooms there was no sign of occupation or damage, but in the small closet off the kitchen a rug had been torn to shreds and was clearly the makings of a nest. Pine martens, I had heard, were tending to come out of the wild, to feed from litter-bins and even to occupy uninhabited houses. Druim was evidently much to the liking of a pair settling into domesticity. It was sad. They would have to be caught.

I wondered what the 'old lady' of Druim, as she was known, would have made of this intrusion. Such a thing would never have occurred in her day, of course. All the little houses contained their families of humans. She and her husband had worked the croft land adjoining the house. Many times she had walked the path to the little well, where a minute fish lived and kept the water pure. She had tended herbs for the soup in her tiny garden plot. A strict Sabbatarian, she would admonish a boy for whistling on a Sunday. The people of Abriachan, in keeping with their character, had mostly gone over to the Free Church at the Disruption. This had meant many a long walk to a church service of their liking, sometimes the outing taking up the whole day, with hunger driving the boys to chew on raw turnips from the fields on the way home. But a strict regime does build character. The 'old lady' and her husband spoke only Gaelic but they knew all about the intrusion of the English and what it meant. Often, on a summer afternoon, they would sit on a bench at the end of their house, beside the road. As the children came up on their way from school, they would ask to be shown the reading books and to be helped to say and understand the words.

She was a story-teller, the old lady, and her granddaughter, Eona Macnicol, has inherited the gift. In English she tells her tales, and beautiful they are. One, called 'A Window Westward', tells how, after her grandmother died, her grandfather, in his old age, came to live with her family in Inverness. He had every care, but was restless and disturbed. Only when they made a window in the west wall of their town house so that he could look in the direction of his beloved bit of country did he settle. His granddaughter has given us many precious things for the Abriachan collection—many photographs, a porridge bowl, books, a hand-woven blanket, the real things of life.

In her imaginative book of short stories, all centred on Abriachan, called *The Hallowe'en Hero*, she talks of her grandfather like this:

But grandpa must follow the course of the Tallurach burn, far up till it winds free of bushes and comes out thin, clear on the open moor. It is a bare landscape, quintessential, austere. There is a hill face, veiling itself at times with mist like some holy mountain. There is a small reed-fringed lochan where waterfowl cry. And there is the moor, with a cold sweet air blowing over its bog myrtle and heather. Hill, lochan and moor. The three. And that is all.

There grandpa's solitary croft lies. His forefathers wrested it from the moor. They scratched out little squares and lifted off the heather and went through the soil beneath, sifting out by hand every individual stone! Thin oats for food and thin barley for drink grew as best they could against the wind. There were potatoes and turnips and a little grassland forever being encroached upon by heather and bulrushes.

Above the croft the cottage stands, twin rowan trees growing by the gable and one wild rose bush. A path of flat stones lead through the swampy land down to the well. The well has three stones for walls, a fourth stone for its roof, with fern sprouting between them. And in it lives a fish, a tiny priestess keeping the water clear.

This is his world, his universe: he has no identity apart from it.

The story of Druim was set to continue. The man who had bought it along with the old schoolmaster's house and who was happy for it to continue to be part of the museum project died quite suddenly in England. His son was not inclined to continue the connection with the Highlands and the place was sold.

Reconstruction is the name of the game, of course. If only it were done in the style appropriate to the environment. The old stone houses with roofs of thatch or slate fitted perfectly into the landscape. But too often they are turned into what could pass for suburban dwellings, complete with mock facade and patio.

At Druim the old steading remains. The path to the well is overgrown with plantings of conifer. The plenishings from the house—the table, the chairs, pots, crockery, beds and bedding—and the implements from the steading, all had to be removed and put in store. When the builders moved in, the little garden, which we had replanted with herbs and flowers, those the old people remembered seeing there, all

Mr Donald Fraser, Eona Macnicol's grandfather, at Druim

disappeared under loads of rubble. I managed to rescue some feverfew, which seeds all over the schoolhouse garden now and which I can happily pass on to friends. I often think of the old lady of Druim curing a headache as she chewed on a handful of the aromatic leaves. I missed my walks up to the place, to tidy the house or tend the garden or to take round a party of visitors eager for a glimpse of the old way of life, to assess its value, to compare it with life today.

But the old way has, of course, to change as the new way moves in. People who had come to live in the area now had children of school age. A mini-bus was coming to collect them in the morning to take them to a school down on the main road, a country school still, with about 20 pupils. There, they have all the equipment that modern technology can provide. They meet children from a near-urban area, they exchange ideas with them, compare notes on life-styles. Inevitably, contacts with the roots of the home environment are minimal. Summer evenings and times of holiday may be spent nearby, but the car makes access to the town Sports Centre an easy 15-minute drive away. Even the shinty-pitch needs 15 minutes car-time, in the other direction, westward towards the glen. Orienteering, too, is organised elsewhere. Kite-flying, bike-riding in summer, sledging or skiing in a winter snow-spell can be enjoyed right from the doorstep. But the idea that the fields and hills surrounding them were once the providers of the means of living is an alien one to most of the children. Bread and oatcakes come package-wrapped from the supermarket, milk is delivered in bottles in the early hours. Heather and rushes are overtaking the fields, the hills grow rows of conifers. Some sheep are grazed, though they lack access to the healthy hill-ground. A few children take part in a family activity of gathering and feeding the flock, even helping at the dipping and clipping. But there are now no cattle-beasts, no milk cows and so no calves to feed, no dairying to learn. The milling of oats, the making of butter and cheese, is something to read about in a Project book.

It's sad to see the old work ethic go, along with early rising, hard-backed chairs, home-made food, neighbourly ceilidhs. With machines taking over the work-place—the office, the factory, the farm—it is clearly becoming unreasonable to expect full-time employment for all the children when they reach maturity. Hence, I suppose, the building of so many leisure complexes, aquadomes, sports centres, theme parks and so on. School, at least the classroom, is perhaps the one place where it can still be considered 'fun' to work at something till you get it right—say, to calculate the cost of building a garden pool, to draw an accurate map of the way to a favoured picnic spot, to write a description of something of interest seen on an outing, to translate a letter from a pen-pal in another country. The relevance of learning to living can put a shine on school work.

I think some notion of the simplicity of the old way of life may rub off on today's children, particularly if they have the opportunity of talking and listening to some of the older native people. Work was hard, but a lot of it was shared. There was always time for a hearty laugh. Welfare was assured on a neighbourly basis. Officialdom was largely mistrusted. One's door was never locked, for someone might need shelter. There was nothing to tempt a thief, in any case. The only recorded instance of a stranger having to knock and be refused instant entry occurred, not so very long ago, in a remote part of the north, when a soldier, strayed on manoeuvres, came to the house of an elderly woman. 'A soldier?' she said, doubtfully. 'Well, I'm sorry. The last time they were here, I'm told they wore red coats and they did a lot of harm. Wait you there.' Moments later she handed him a dram and an oatcake, through the half-opened door, and set him on his way. So memory dies hard.

Contemporary in-fighting in many parts of the world, as seen on our television screen, bears a clear resemblance to the Jacobite days, with their many battles. The political aftermath has many similarities, too, with repression, confiscation and other drastic measures carried out in the bid to rule. *Plus ça change*...Jacobites and Redcoats made a better game than Cowboys and Indians for the children of these parts. How could it be otherwise, when in one of the oldest and more inaccessible places lived a descendant of one of the seven men of Glenmoriston, those seven men who sheltered the Prince in a cave high in the hills, risking their lives daily, and steadfastly refusing to accept the ransom money placed upon his head. There is ample scope for a history lesson at a stone's throw from our doors here. Let's hope compilers of curricula will allow flexibility and scope to include variations in approach, so that matters studied may be relevant to the childrens' situations. The swotting-up of innumerable Acts of Parliament, even learning the story of the American Civil War, for instance, would seem to have little bearing on life in the Highlands yesterday or today. Tell a child the story of his own country and he begins to understand who he is. This is family history in an extended sense. Let him hear the myths and legends as well as the stark facts. That was what helped the children of long-past ages to grow in stature. Let them absorb the reality of their surroundings, too. Show them a flower, a rowan growing out of the rock, a stag as he roars defiance at the world, an eagle soaring, a canopy of stars.

So many times I saw that look of stark wonder on the faces of the children who came out here from the town. To find that things grow and die and grow again, that a bee-sting can be easily cured and that you don't harm a creature that gives you honey, that foxes have to live, though the loss of a lamb is hard: these discoveries and many more led, I think, to an inkling of what the world is about, to the tentative beginnings of wisdom.

There are signs here, now, of a revival of interest in some of the traditional pursuits of Highland people. Children are playing shinty, many are learning to play traditional music on clarsach, fiddle, accordion, recorder and penny whistle, to sing the old songs and to dance the old reels and dances. All this is done, of course, in the context of today, of telecommunication, of video, of electronic and computer technique. So much, nowadays, is recorded, filed away in tidy packaging. There is no recording of the bruises on the shinty-player's legs as he's carried away in triumph from the field, of the sweat on the brow of the fiddler as he plays his heart out at the ceilidh! These must be experienced in the raw.

Song and dance have always been a natural part of people's lives the world over. They reflect the underlying realities of hope, fear, conflict, love, endeavour, loss. This context is the one that children may glimpse if they grow to it from their early years.

More importantly, there is, here, a continuing of the traditional sense of community. Work cannot be shared as it was in former times, as peoples' lives now vary greatly, but the old ways of helping life along are there and the children are encouraged to take part in them. There is a sharing of care for the old and alone, for the very young and vulnerable, a ready hand at the cutting of firewood, the weeding of a garden plot, the feeding of cats, dogs and chickens. There is still the assurance that help is there should it be needed.

As more people moved into the area, some from more populous places where social life was active, a movement to re-establish the village hall as a centre for gatherings gradually emerged. It had always been understood that the collection housed there would be removed should there be a demand for the place to revert to its original status. So, one December day, a party of volunteers arrived, with wagons and trailers, and all the well-loved objects, with documents, photographs and tools, were put in store.

Grants were obtained for the refurbishing of the hall. Toilets, electricity and hot water were installed. Much hard work was put in on a voluntary basis—painting, repairing windows and woodwork, partitioning and so on. Meetings are held there now, a recently formed youth group pursues various activities, there is some country dancing. A winter ceilidh and a summer barbecue are popular. At ceilidhs we sing the old songs, listen to the old music, dance a reel or two. For those of us who remember the fireside ceilidhs of older times, when you met on a winter's night, happy to see half a dozen neighbours, to exchange news and views, to enjoy a dram and a cup of tea, to sing a song if the spirit took you, maybe to tell an old story heard many times before, while the women knitted, the men smoked, and the children dozed off in a corner, for us few the public ceilidh has more the feel and structure of a concert or entertainment. As a social occasion it is enjoyable and people do like to get together in numbers, but it lacks the intimacy of the fireside gatherings. Perhaps we came nearest to that when we met round the open fire in the old schoolroom.

Chapter
Eighteen

I began then to dream, to think seriously even, about the possibility of re-instating the school as a centre of learning, in a new form. I could visualise one room as the schoolroom of 1875...On the first of February of that year Alexander Maclean, a young man of twenty-five, was appointed headmaster in the new school. What do we know of him? He had trained for a year at the College in Moray House in Edinburgh and taught for four years at nearby Glenconvinth School. There were about seventy pupils on the roll. His salary was £85 a year. He had an assistant who was paid £20 a year. Fees paid by the parents were 1s 6d to 3s 6d per quarter. There is no record of the subjects taught, but it is likely they were similar to those taught by his predecessor in the old school, Mr McGillivray.

These were (for 85 pupils)—

Reading: 85
Writing: 50
Arithmetic: 50
Grammar: 24
Geography: 20
Sewing: 20

There were 40 in the Sabbath school and 26 were taught Gaelic.

How the Gaelic teaching fitted into the curriculum is not clear. Children of today, coming to visit, might come to understand and appreciate the difficulties their forebears, perhaps their own grandparents, had in acquiring knowledge. No flickering computer screens brought them fascinating glimpses of things in far-off parts, but they did learn how to deal with the things that immediately concerned them—getting to school on a day of drifting snow, in leaking boots, for a start. Then, on the way home, in summer, they learned which plants were sweet to chew on and how to guddle small trout from under stones in the burn to take home for tea. There would have been jobs to cope with before and after school—bringing in the cow for milking or washing tatties in the ice-cold water of the burn. Holidays were not long and punishments could be harsh. Taking the strap on fingers reddened with chilblains in winter must have been an agony of pain. But lessons had to be learnt. The well-being of the school and of the master depended on scholarly achievement in the days of 'payment by results'. Truancy was penalised, parents being fined or even imprisoned when a grant for good attendance was at stake.

The children, looking round the old classroom and comparing it with their own brightly-lit, well-furnished premises, would shudder at the thought of being educated there, though when the 'new' school was completed and Mr Maclean arrived, it was regarded as a palace.

Today's children could have a lesson in the old style, sit at desks, copy some magnificent writing from the blackboard, do 'spellings', recite the multiplication table, add, subtract, divide 'mentally' (no fingers to be used!). Books being in short supply, they would listen to stories and poems the master read to them. Stories, tales of 'olden times', when their forebears lived and died, would make their history lesson. The poems they would have to write down and learn 'by heart'. Singing, with the master and his magic tuning fork, would be a relaxation, but a disciplined one, with no excuse for wrong notes or giggles. A dunce's cap or a flick of the tawse were always to be dreaded, but a glint of approval in the master's eye was something to be prized.

After a while the children might well be surprised at the extent to which they'd been 'stretched', pleased with their achievement or eager to do better. It could be more than 'play-acting'. It could be an eye-opener to those watching and those taking part.

For the adult visitors there could be talks and discussions on the story of education yesterday and today. There would be a special welcome for people from rural schools abroad, who could exchange experiences with teachers in these parts. In the old 'Infants' Room' a small library could be used for private study.

How to get children to fulfil their potential, to live life to the full, to adapt, to communicate, isn't that what it's all about? When we think back to the appalling conditions in which schoolmasters lived in the days of the Parish Schools and the early days of those of the S.S.P.C.K., while yet managing to produce many 'lads o' pairts' who contributed much to the world, the problems of today's educationists do seem less significant. Books and equipment were hard to come by then. Even as late as the 1920s there were many practical difficulties to be overcome in the running of the school here. The building itself, a product of the Victorian age, was made to withstand the onslaught of storm—rain, gale, snow—unlike some modern schools, with roofs that blow off or leak. But there were other problems. The water supply, which comes from a spring high in the hill, was often giving out, owing to choked or damaged pipes. Many times the Log Book records the summoning of plumbers. The dry closets had to be emptied and cleaned by the headmaster, for an additional £6 a year. Not till 1928 was water installed, after the unsanitary conditions were reported to the health authorities.

Over the years, education in Scotland, from the days of the Church administration, has tended to be academically inclined. Early schoolmasters were often 'stickit ministers', or even part-time students for the ministry. Gifted children were favoured and often scant attention paid to the less able. This is not so today. Pendulums swing high. But recent investigations into teaching have shown that a return to more formal methods is needed. Children taught in the old-fashioned way, sitting at desks, in rows, pay more attention to the spoken word, learn more, retain more, than those sitting at tables, moving round the room and talking a good deal. In this school of thought education is, perhaps less child-centred, more teacher-centred. In fact, the most important person is the teacher. When this is acknowledged the children benefit.

Today, education is very much in the political arena. To a certain extent it always was. In our age we need skilled operatives to ensure success in the ever-more competitive market-places of the world. To help increase the speed of economic growth would appear to be the aim in educational reform. We must hope that there are teachers perceptive enough to ensure that the well-trained, industrious people coming out of the schools of the future will also have had their minds stretched to include the appreciation of poetry, music and drama, and have acquired the ability to discriminate between the good, the bad and the indifferent in the arts as well as in modes of behaviour.

Education and its problems is now an everyday topic of conversation, as it is becoming apparent that more and more children are leaving school unable to read, write or count. The size of classes is often discussed. In the old school in Abriachan, in the 1920s, the number of pupils in the 'big' room was 70. Today, classes of 30 are anathema. In 1866 members of the Argyll Commission, investigating the state of education at the time, wrote 'a good master is quite able to interest and teach 80 or 100 boys in the earlier years of their course'.

In my experience, it is the ability of the teacher to teach that matters.

A SCHOOL IN THE HILLS

Children will listen to someone who clearly knows and likes what he is talking about and can communicate his enthusiasm. All the equipment really needed is a blackboard and some chalk. Yes, chalk and talk again! Books for follow-up work at home, are, of course, essential. There must be respite from those hours of television. This, supplemented by time spent outside the classroom, looking at things, doing things, perhaps digging a garden, planting trees, clearing rubbish, would keep them in touch with true reality, which is so much more satisfying than the virtual kind. Computers are a necessary part of modern equipment, maybe, but still they are only machines. They can calculate, if properly fed, can inform and compare, but they can't discuss things with you, answer your unexpected questions, crack a joke with you, give you a dressing-down if you need one.

Our old school in the hills here, with its high windows and its dusty floors, its outside toilets and its stone-strewn playground would obviously fall far below the standard deemed essential to meet the needs of the modern child. Yet it still retains the feel of the children, of the headmasters, of dedicated assistant teachers and anxious parents, of Inspectors, Attendance Officers, visiting ministers and landlords, of all the human beings who frequented it over the years. And there are no ghosts, no unhappy hauntings, only, I hope, a prospect of its future as the interpreter of its past.